LIVING BEFORE DYING

New Directions in Anthropology

General Editor: **Jacqueline Waldren**, *Institute of Social and Cultural Anthropology, University of Oxford*

Twentieth-century migration, modernization, technology, tourism, and global communication have had dynamic effects on group identities, social values and conceptions of space, place, and politics. This series features new and innovative ethnographic studies concerned with these processes of change.

For a full volume listing, please see back matter

LIVING BEFORE DYING

Imagining and Remembering Home

Janette Davies

berghahn
NEW YORK · OXFORD
www.berghahnbooks.com

First published in 2017 by
Berghahn Books
www.berghahnbooks.com

Library of Congress Cataloging-in-Publication Data
Names: Davies, Janette, author.
Title: Living before dying : imagining and remembering home / Janette
Davies.
Description: New York : Berghahn Books, [2017] | Series: New directions in
anthropology ; volume 41 | Includes bibliographical references.
Identifiers: LCCN 2017014975 (print) | LCCN 2017030588 (ebook) | ISBN
9781785336157 (e-book) | ISBN 9781785336140 (hbk) |
ISBN 9781789201307 (pbk)
Subjects: LCSH: Nursing homes--Anthropological aspects. | Nursing
homes--Sociological aspects. | Dementia--Patients--Care.
Classification: LCC RA997 (ebook) | LCC RA997 .D37 2017 (print) | DDC
362.16--dc23
LC record available at https://lccn.loc.gov/2017014975

British Library Cataloguing in Publication Data
A catalogue record for this book is available from the British Library

ISBN: 978-1-78533-614-0 (hardback)
ISBN: 978-1-78920-130-7 (paperback)
ISBN: 978-1-78533-615-7 (ebook)

CONTENTS

∼⁕∼

FOREWORD

Lord Nigel Crisp

In this interesting and valuable study, the author brings an anthropologist's eye to the minutiae of life in a large residential home.

We see the way in which residents behave, how they interact with relatives and each other and the different behaviours of the men and women. We listen in, too, on the conversations between the author and her co-workers as they share their stories and respond to the residents and to pressures of their work.

Health and care services throughout the western world have been trying over recent years to personalise care and make sure that every individual receives the care they need – and is treated as an individual with preferences and expectations as well as physical needs. It is part of a wider trend that sees health as not just being a physical concept but as embracing well-being and concerned with all the bio-psycho-social aspects of life. It is something that comes more naturally to a trained nurse, like the author, than to most health workers and care assistants.

This is a trend epitomised by Maureen Bisognano who, as president of the Institute for Healthcare Improvement, said we must move away from asking a patient *What's the matter with you?* to asking *What matters to you?* This profound change recognises not only that people have their own individual habits, expectations and preferences but also, at the physical level, that every disease – be it Parkinson's or dementia – manifests itself differently in different individuals.

Janette Davies takes us into a world of old age and frailty where people find themselves thrust together with others whom they would never have been close to in earlier life. She tells us of old ladies who are appalled by the behaviour of some of the men and unable to hide their disgust at, in some cases, the lack of hygiene and anti-social behaviours. We also see men who want more than this passive life and find it hard to cope with restrictions and sometimes, because of their medical condition, behave with excessive lack of inhibition. They all bring with them their personal history and the learned habits of a lifetime.

This is a world where in extreme old age people are having to learn how to – or at least how to cope with – living communally. It is also a life where there are times of great joy and hope. There are trips to the outside world that stimulate and excite, bringing memories to savour and relive, and treats of cakes, sherry or hairdressing. It is a world where the caregivers wield great power and set the tone and atmosphere. We hear of great kindnesses – of patient women treating their charges with the delicacy and compassion they might give to their own mothers, talking and listening as they do their work. There are moments of thoughtfulness that transform a person's day and make the reader catch their breath, but there are also moments of casual unconcern where tasks are done without thought, completed but not valued. Where one carer will leave residents in their baths for longer so that they can enjoy the physical pleasure, another will hurry them through to get the job done.

Offstage from these intimate human dramas, strings are pulled by unseen managers whose actions can enhance or damage the quality of this time spent in *Living before Dying*. Further away still are the policies and policymakers who shape the whole environment through regulation, oversight and funding. Meanwhile, the politicians and the wider population are still adjusting to our ageing population and the profound changes it is bringing. Already one in six people over the age of eighty-five spend some time in residential care. We don't yet know how we as a society are going to cope – the problem is becoming well understood but not the solutions. How will we improve care and/or create alternatives to this kind of residential care?

This book does not attempt to offer solutions, nor does it judge the merits and disadvantages of the institution that has opened its doors so generously to the scrutiny of the author. The great value of the book, however, is that it takes the vital first steps towards solutions by anatomising the reality in human terms, helping us to see what really happens – the good and the bad – within the walls of an institution where one's personal life and the *imagining and remembering of home* are lived out in a very public space.

This book will no doubt be read by anthropologists and academics but it should also be read by health and social care workers as well as policymakers at all levels who are thinking deeply about these dilemmas and planning for a future of personalised rather than institutionalised care – whether in homes like this one or some other sort of facility.

Lord Nigel Crisp was Chief Executive of the NHS in England and Permanent Secretary of the UK Department of Health from 2000 to 2006.

Acknowledgements

My decision to publish the findings of this study on residents in a nursing home only after all the residents had died was made early in the research; all these people are now deceased. In life they knew of my gratitude for their presence in the study and their relatives (some of whom have kept in touch) are aware of my immense appreciation for sharing their family biographies and narratives with me.

Anonymity and change of Christian name was conferred on the residents. Some actual names are used, honouring the request of relatives whose hope was that the dignity lost within the experience of dementia would be conferred on their kin by being named in print.

Where informed consent could not be articulated by the person suffering with dementia, relatives gladly consented to the family member being observed and interviewed, and to them I owe much gratitude. Staff and employees at the nursing home are also thanked for their readiness to participate and be observed in their daily tasks, day by day for over a year.

The Bodleian Library, University of Oxford provided space for me to write and use their valued reserve sections for my texts, especially The China Centre Library located in the grounds of St Hugh's College and the Philosophy and Theology Faculties Library located in the old Radcliffe Infirmary building. Ralph Bates, librarian at Oxford Centre for Mission Studies, facilitated a quiet workspace for me over the years, while his skills as a proof reader proved invaluable.

Sarah-Jane White of the Institute of Human Sciences, University of Oxford helped edit a decade's worth of newspaper articles on the increased plight of elderly people during this study. Our friendship was formed by the residence in the nursing home of her great-aunt who features in this study. Dr Kate Tomas, a post-doctoral scholar in theology at the University of Oxford, and Anne Meeker, one-time undergraduate at St Hugh's College,

Oxford, provided invaluable assistance on formatting the chapters and references. Their youthful enthusiasm for my subject kept up the momentum!

Dr Nick Robins and the Revd (Dr) Judith Thomas both offered advice and encouragement, while Revd Hedley Feast, retired chaplain at the John Radcliffe Hospital Oxford, shared my concerns regarding holistic care for our elders. All colleagues at International Gender Studies, Lady Margaret Hall encouraged me in the analysis and writing up of this book. My school friend Dee Cormack ably assisted with the literature search on care of older people, while other nurses from our Cheltenham class of '68 reminded me of the fun and sorrows of nursing older people. Margaret Maguire, my sister, a former nurse and currently an organiser of care in the community, was an invaluable source of information and encouragement. Jeff, my husband, knows of my love and gratitude for his unfailing support and because thanks in English are not expressive enough, I say thank you in Welsh – *Diolch yn Fawr.*

INTRODUCTION

For my part I would rather not be old so long than be old before my time. The
weakness of childhood, the impetuosity of youth, the seriousness of middle
life, the maturity of old age – each bears some of Nature's fruit, which must be
garnered in its own season.
—Cicero, 44 BC

In the last few decades, the care of frail older people within UK society has
been highlighted as careering from one crisis to another due to the cost of
provision of social services and nursing care. These crises, drawn attention
to in the media and in academic research, have become heightened since the
global financial recession of 2008. National government cutbacks resulted in
a decline in public funding by local authorities, the National Health Service
(NHS) and social services for frail and sick older people receiving care in the
community. During the process of identifying the need for anthropological
research in this area, I concentrated on combining my background in nursing with that of my training as an anthropologist. The convergence of these
two disciplines resulted in anthropological research being undertaken where
health professionals and health auxiliaries were at work. Aware of a task-
focused culture within nursing, I also wished to see if this was evident within
nursing home practice in the UK. It had been apparent during my years
working as a nurse in developing countries, as well as within the nursing
profession in England, especially and notably while training in nursing and
midwifery. According to Menzies' (1970) early study in a large hospital that
endeavoured to develop new methods of performing tasks within nursing,
'ritual task-performance' exists to spare staff the anxiety of making decisions.
Over forty years later, the process is still being debated within nursing,
centring on the need to move from task-oriented to science-based practice.
Ten years working as a part-time staff nurse commencing in 2000 at the

Oxford University Hospitals NHS Trust (OUH), a world-renowned centre of clinical excellence and one of the largest NHS teaching trusts in the UK, enabled me to see whether or not this ideology was put into practice.

In the early 1990s, after finishing an MSc degree in medical anthropology and then a Master of Studies in social anthropology, and before undertaking doctoral studies, I worked for a nurse employment agency across the county and was willing to perform weekend night shifts in either residential nursing homes, the children's hospital or industry. Because of persistent staff shortages in many nursing homes, work was readily offered and accepted as my ideas for research in such a setting began to formulate. It was during many shifts in the nursing homes that the need to conduct anthropological research in such institutions became evident and, in particular, the need to analyse the minutiae of life within these homes. Anthropological study within care homes could inform as to the presence or absence of a quality of life both for residents and employees. The term 'quality of life' is used in guidelines for managers and staff of residential nursing homes (Residential Forum 1996; Philpot 2008; DEMOS 2014) as well as studies among older people, as will be shown later. The home studied was chosen because of its size, with over seventy residents, thirty staff and a large enough suite of buildings for the researcher to be able to conduct a study involving participant observation, without being too intrusive. Managers at the nursing home as well as the owners gave their permission, and approval was gained from the Local Authority Ethics Committee. Subsequent research undertaken with colleagues in the Oxford University Hospitals NHS Trust highlighted the recurring delays in the discharge of older patients, particularly when the media took up the descriptive but derogatory terms of 'bed-blockers' and 'bed-blocking'. This research into delayed discharge from hospital resulted in publications illustrating the use of a new (to the UK) measure of function and cognitive assessment of independence of older patients known as the Alpha FIM (Hinkle et al. 2010). What was so significant in the use of this score/measure by health professionals was the ability to use the results to determine cognition or its lack in the older patient and thus make predictions of admission/discharge outcomes.

In recent decades, newspaper articles have consistently highlighted a growing discontent within British society regarding its treatment of older people, and particularly the frail and sick person in need of social services and nursing care. These newspaper stories criticised the various governments, especially the Conservative government of the 1990s and 2000s, for the continuous cutbacks in funding for social service and health service provision. The suspicion of rationing care and treatment for older people is never far from the surface of these reports in the daily press. In order to set the social context and climate for the study conducted within the nursing home, a summary of newspaper articles from the past twenty years is presented by way of introduction to the public's perceptions of treatment and care management of older people, namely sick and frail elders within British society. The newspaper headlines selected are as follows.

'Where do I want to live when I'm old? – unless we start a national debate now, our own old age could be bleak'. The photograph with this article shows a staff member and resident sitting in a home for older people; the photo caption says 'good homes are hard to find' (Aslet, *The Times* 1994).

'Home Sweet Home' – caring for the elderly is big business where fortunes have already been made (Kane and Waples, *The Sunday Times* 1994).

'Families given warning on costs of care' – old people and the chronic sick are not entitled to long-term care under the NHS may result in patients being forced into private nursing homes (Laurance, *The Times* 1995).

'Scheme helps elderly stay put' (Editor, *Oxford Mail* 1995). An Oxfordshire district council, with social services and a housing trust, plan to enable older people to stay in their homes by offering advice and practical help with repairs and improvements.

'Granny flats to be charged council tax' – court blow for the elderly (Horsnell, *The Times* 1995). This front-page news story followed the High Court's ruling that families providing 'granny flats' for relatives would have to pay two council tax bills. Anticipated public outrage was addressed in an Editorial entitled 'A tax on caring – keeping the elderly at home should not be penalised' (Editorial, *The Times* 1995). Within the same edition of the newspaper, the political correspondent wrote of the Labour government's plan for a Royal Commission to report on care of the elderly and other vulnerable groups (Sherman and Frean, *The Times* 1995).

'Community Care Act forces ailing pensioners to spend life-savings on health fees – woman aged 79 has paid £100,000 for husband's nursing'. She kept a pamphlet dated 1948, describing the launch of the NHS, and on spending their savings stressed that her 'contract' had been broken even though they paid tax all their lives (Cox, *The Times* 1995). This example was included with similar case histories, in light of the government's decision to introduce harsh means-testing for pensioners, the front-page headlines reading: 'Battle to stop elderly losing their homes. Major aims to end penalty for thrift' (Murray and Wood, *The Times* 1995).

'Nursing home operators look for healthier future'. Pending government proposals for people to insure themselves for ageing and long-term care, the top ten public companies providing residential care for older people are highlighted (Suzman and Rich, *Financial Times* 1996).

'Gently, gingerly… asks how rehabilitation services can be revitalised for elderly patients hustled out of hospital'. As wards and hospitals for older people in need of rehabilitation close down, more people who could be discharged back to their homes are being discharged permanently to residential care homes (Rickford, *The Guardian* 1997).

'What the eyes don't see. By institutionalising our loved ones, are we surrendering them to the enemy within?' Grant writes of the guilt felt at placing her mother in a residential home and the worry over the possibility of abuse (Grant, *The Guardian* 1997).

'Protection for the elderly' was written after *The Sunday Times* posed the question, 'Who cares for the plight of Britain's elderly people?' Sack loads of mail, e-mail messages and telephone calls told of neglect and poor care in many nursing homes and residential homes around Britain (Editorial, *The Sunday Times* 1997).

'Elderly must wait on care'. In light of the Royal Commission on funding for long-term care of elderly people, this article highlights the response. The overall recommendation is that long-term nursing care for older people should be free as it is in the NHS. The government is criticised for conniving to delay any legislation until 2001, while an editorial in the same newspaper suggests that the conclusions of the report will bankrupt the nation (Sherman and Frean, *The Times* 1999; Editorial, *The Times* 1995).

'Let the old eat what they want, says Leith'. Urging nursing homes 'to adopt a more flexible approach to meal times', Prue Leith emphasised 'the social significance of communal eating', giving an example of a ninety-year-old woman who was miserable at meal times. She was given poached eggs on wholemeal toast by a twenty-year-old staff member whereas all her long life she had eaten fry-ups and white bread. Leith gave a 'spirited defence' for the woman to choose what she wanted (Frean, *The Times* 1999).

'Garden where memories grow'. A nursing home garden in Scotland planned to 'unlock patients with dementia from their secret world'. Staff found that a physically fit man in his eighties with dementia had been a keen gardener, so they created a vegetable garden for him whereupon he 'instinctively' knew what to do when gardening which drew him back to a familiar world, giving his life new meaning (Elliott, *The Times* 1999).

'NHS has failed elderly, says damning report' (Abraham, *The Times* 2011).

'Care for the elderly is a casualty of over-pressed nursing' (Letters to the Editor, *The Times* 2011).

'Without care – poor financial management is not all that is wrong with British care homes' (Editorial, *The Times* 2011).

'Strategic vision won't fix a leaky lavatory – you can't run a care home on diktats from head office. Bring in the micro-managers and restore some pride' (Purves, *The Times* 2011).

'Midlifers caught between worlds – Sandwich generation cares for parents and children' (Ford, *The Times* 2011).

'Spending on care for the elderly falls by a fifth' (Savage, *The Times* 2011).

'Music offers a path back to reality for dementia sufferers' (Maclean, *The Times* 2012).

'Councils still measuring elderly care in minutes – clock watchers: how councils measure out care in minutes' (Barrow and Coates, *The Times* 2012).

'Dutch approach to dementia is encouraging' (Letters to the Editor, *The Times* 2012a).

'Stop sending patients home late at night, hospitals told' (Smyth, *The Times* 2012).

'The elderly are not bed blockers they are patients' (Bauley, *The Times* 2012).

'Reality of caring for elderly relatives in 21st-century Britain' (Letters to the Editor, *The Times* 2012b).

'Transform care for the elderly, urge charities – final plea to No. 10 to prevent families "picking up pieces"' (Bennett, *The Times* 2012a).

'No. 10 sits on "urgent" care reforms – campaigners are angry after plan to cap costs is delayed' (Bennett, *The Times* 2012b).

'What shall we do with Mother? As the Social Care Bill looks at ways to cope with an ageing society, the strain isn't just about money. What if your elderly parent drives you mad?' (Scott, *The Times* 2012).

'Elderly would rather lose fuel cash than bus passes' (Moody, *The Times* 2012).

'250,000 elderly Britons alone and lonely at Christmas' (Bennett, *The Times* 2012c).

'Put your parents out to grass in hi-tech garden shed – welcome to the granny pod' (Blakeley, *The Times* 2012).

'Care home measures may not halt crisis – the cost of caring for the elderly is now being addressed – but is it too late?' (Editor, *The Times* 2013).

'Cruel short visits deprive elderly of dignity and care – more Councils tell staff to stay just 15 minutes' (Smyth, *The Times* 2013a).

'Overstretched care workers "put elderly in danger"' (Bennett, *The Times* 2013).

'Who will look after you when you are old? To avoid loneliness in later years, don't look to the penniless State – start planning now' (Thompson, *The Times* 2013).

'Plenty of reasons to laugh in this happy, loving home – an Abbeyfield Society residence for the elderly that offers friendly care and banishes boredom' (Law, *The Times* 2013).

'Heston helps older patients get a healthy appetite back' (Smyth, *The Times* 2013b).

'Barely legal – Britain's approach to caring for the elderly is a national disgrace' (Editorial, *The Times* 2014).

'Old people turn to "lonely" care homes only as a final resort' (Bennett, *The Times* 2014).

'It's horrible to say, but dementia is a writer's gift'. Emma Healey won the Costa First Novel award with a mystery about memory loss (Wilson, *The Times* 2015).

'Elderly care home residents auctioned off by councils on "eBay-style" website'. Care homes in the area are invited to bid to offer the older person a home (Editorial, *Daily Telegraph* 2015).

'Woman cannot find care home after allegations of ill treatment'. A daughter claimed that complaints she made about her mother's treatment in care homes and hospitals made it difficult to find a residential home willing to take her in (Lay, *The Times* 2016).

With these illustrative articles in mind, I turn to a historical overview of the allocation of residential care in British society and the measures to reform care therein.

Reconsidering Residential Care

Long-term residential care for older people is not a recent initiative; from the late 1940s until the 1980s, long-term residential care for older people was provided for at the foundation of the NHS in 1948. The 'chronic-sick' prior to this were housed in public assistance institutions that were integrated into the newly formed NHS. The earlier institutions have their origins in the Poor Relief Act of 1601, where all parishes were responsible for housing the poor, the sick and older people in 'custodial institutions'. The act distanced itself from the more recognisable forms of punishing paupers in the Tudor system and aimed for methods of correction. The characteristics of these 'workhouses' live on in people's memories, especially for some of the very old residents in this study. Buildings survive that are commonly referred to as the 'workhouse', even though the NHS was instigated over sixty years ago. Prior to the Poor Relief Act, and before the dissolution of the monasteries, hospitals, which included care for the elderly, were run by religious institutions, which in the third and fourth centuries were known as *'gerontochia'*, established by the Church to care for elderly people (Townsend 1964). What is significant about residential homes in the late twentieth and early twenty-first centuries compared to earlier eras, however, is that they are not seen as custodial. Also, although some state-run homes still exist, an increasing number from the 1990s onwards are business ventures first, in that they are privately run and emerged in the push for privatisation by successive UK governments.

Coinciding with this development is the changing demography of the client group and the increasing incidence of dementia within that group. The Community Care Act was the catalyst for this process of change. It generated significant players under these reforms, involving the voluntary and private sectors in the delivery of that care (Department of Health 1990). The narratives of the care assistants who worked in the home also mention this change in emphasis, consistently describing their workload as becoming 'heavier' even though residents are increasingly more frail. Population statistics for England and Wales highlight a change in the age of people in residential care. Although 16% of people aged over eighty-five in the UK live in care homes, the resident care home population is ageing – in 2011, people aged over eighty-five represented 59.2% of the older care home population compared to 56.5% in 2001 (Age UK 2015: 14).

Some of the earlier newspaper articles above were published during the implementation of the National Health Service and Community Care Act 1990, enacted in 1993 (Department of Health 1990), within which the aim of community care was to give people the opportunity to live as independently as possible in their own homes or in other 'home' settings such as sheltered housing or care/nursing homes.

During the years of planning for the introduction of the Care Act Reforms, which became the Care Act (Local Government Association 2014), there was a continued need to reiterate that care and entitlement to care be clarified and strengthened to safeguard the social care needs for older people as well as the prioritised nursing care. A significant aspect of care of people in the community, either in their own homes or in residential homes, is 'needs assessment', considered by many families to be harsh and intrusive. The social services appointed care managers to undertake these assessments upon implementation of the Community Care Act in 1990 (personal communication with Sally Brodhurst, Joint Commissioning Manager, Oxford Social Services and Health Authority) and it is this aspect of care and its service provision that is highlighted by journalists. The Care Act aimed to implement 'the most significant reform of care and support in more than 60 years', placing the people, their relatives and their carers in command of their own care and provision. The Care Act claims: 'For the first time, the Act will put a limit on the amount anyone will have to pay towards the costs of their care' (Lamb 2014), though relatives stress this is not always true in reality.

Residential care in the decades prior to the 1990s was provided by local authorities and social services departments, and had its origins in the 1948 National Assistance Act, under which terms the local authorities had to provide a residential place for anyone who because of age, illness or other reasons was seen to be in need of care and attention. What was hoped for, and in some ways achieved, was the replacing of the old workhouses with modern purpose-built residential homes. Like others since Townsend's major study, *The Last Refuge*, this research continues in the footsteps of his major investigation of long-term residential care published in the 1950s. One of his observations was that due to postwar austerity and the lack of financial capital, many of the planned residential homes were not built. Around the country, former workhouses modified to modern social needs continued in the provision of residential care for older, sick people. In Townsend's study, some of the residents within these homes were seen to be able-bodied and it was Townsend's work that did much to highlight their plight. Today, a care home, once termed a nursing home, can be registered to accept both people needing residential care as well as those needing nursing care, meaning there are able-bodied as well as frail, sick residents. The home in this study is dual registered and is popular with people seeking residential care and especially with relatives because nursing care can be provided if and when needed in the future. However, it was observed that the majority of residents admitted to the home were in need of some nursing care.

In the planning stages between the Community Care Act 1990 and its implementation in 1993, I was one of the researchers conducting a study to assess the need for a greater understanding of the role of housing agencies in community care and their interaction with other providers (Arnold et al. 1993). Acknowledging the importance of adequate housing within community care, the findings suggested that if hidden housing requirements had been adequately addressed, then the situation of countless people ending up in institutional care could have been prevented. My component included researching the housing and community care needs of Bangladeshi elders living in Oxford. The aims were to consider their perceptions of the housing situation as well as their access to social services, and the forward planning for future care needs including the inevitable ups and downs in family and community support.

These research findings showed that the majority of elders wanted their families to care for them, as some were already doing. However, some had doubts that their family would or should provide care at home, even though all totally rejected the idea of residential care, not even considering it as a 'last resort', but did express a need to know what facilities and services existed in order to plan for future short-term respite residential care. With the implementation of care in the community, the older Bangladeshis fulfilled their wish of being cared for by family members with statutory services in their own homes, as borne out by the findings here. No residents were members of any ethnic minority group.

Rural Riverside Setting of the Nursing Home

The nursing home in this study is set in large grounds leading down to the River Thames, located in a tiny hamlet of houses and bungalows, with one public house and a farm, but no shops. Although it is on a country bus route served from a market town less than six miles from the home and another market town eight miles away, the direct bus service is infrequent. A sprawling village on the river nearby is a tourist spot, but the home's greatest contact is with a village that contains a large housing estate and schools one mile from the nursing home.

Many of the staff working at the home live on this housing estate. Although only a mile away from the large housing estate, there is a sense of isolation about the setting of the home, off a main road with extensive grounds leading down to the river. It is this sense of isolation that leads me to describe the home as remote. The setting of the home and isolation from active mainstream life render a remoteness about it, in stark contrast to the busy urban areas and market towns where many of the residents had once lived.

Until the late 1960s, the main building was home to a family who owned and ran a jeweller's shop in a nearby town. It was converted into a residential home for older people run by a doctor and after ten years bought by entrepreneurs who provided larger premises run as a family venture. After two extra wings were added and nursing care was introduced, it was sold to a large nursing home group in the 1980s. This public company was once one of the top ten companies listed in the country (Suzman and Rich 1996). The manager of the home describes it as being a 'home from home' for the residents and their families, and this phrase features in the promotional material. At full capacity, the home takes seventy-four residents, usually around seventeen men and fifty-five women. It is divided into three wings, each with its own sitting rooms, while two have a dining area. One of the wings houses the area where hairdressing and services such as chiropody take place, which therefore serves as a focal point during weekdays. This focal area, which forms an extended dining area, is also close to the manager's office. In the three main lounges of the three wings, there are television sets with the usual choice of channels. In the dining area of one lounge, there is an upright piano. Two of the five lounges have radios, but near the end of the study, with a change of management, a system of piped music to all the sitting areas was installed. One lounge has a large window overlooking the garden and river, and another lounge with eighteen chairs has a glimpse of the garden from one window, where three chairs are located, meaning that the fifteen other chairs only have a view from a window overlooking a narrow alleyway that runs from the garden to an entrance, which visitors use. A third lounge has a long window (along its length) with views to shrubs and part of the main garden. However, this view is only seen by those residents sitting in the chairs facing the window, and not from the six chairs that have their backs to it. A fourth small sitting room with no window was allocated to two residents who smoke cigarettes.

In what was the original building, most of the upstairs rooms have a good view of the grounds, whereas others have only a limited view. Downstairs there are newer single and shared rooms built along what was the front of the original house, and these face the view down to the river. No room in the main house had an en-suite bathroom and toilet, but all had wash-basins and commodes. In two newer extensions, single rooms built with en-suite facilities are allocated predominantly to private, rather than state-funded residents. However, there is a design fault with access to the en-suite bathrooms, in that there is no room to manoeuvre a wheelchair. On looking at the building from the outside, one can distinctly observe a change of purpose from a family home to a residential institution with a change of layout, namely not using what was the house's original main entrance. The kitchen and utility rooms, which would once have been at the back of the house, are now housed along the side. These utility rooms face the main entrance and the drive leading from the main road, but are not observed from the road as two cottages within the property lie alongside. In the design and building of new residential homes, emphasis is now placed on user-friendliness for the residents. This emphasis obviously arose out of trial and error in some of the earlier homes, which added extensively and haphazardly to the original buildings.

Although a private nursing/care home, and belonging at the time of the initial study to a large group of nursing homes, this home cared for residents funded by social services, as well as those self-funded. There are three main sectors providing long-term care in the UK, namely the state-run services such as the local authority or the NHS; the private sector, such as business concerns; and the voluntary sector such as the Church or those for retired musicians/actors. Local authority provision expects residents to contribute to the cost of their care, if they are able, while NHS provision is free at the point of entry (evidence on care of elders to The Royal Commission in Royal College of Nursing 1998; personal communication Maura Buchannan, President, RCN, 2014). It is this that led to the setting up of the Royal Commission to look at the funding for long-term care of the elderly. Its conclusions recommended that nursing care costs should cease to be the responsibility of the resident (Royal Commission on Long Term Care for the Elderly 1999). Over a decade later, Dilnot, Warner and Williams (2011) addressed similar issues of funding long-term care within their phrase 'fairer care funding'.

Demographically, the home is made up of residents aged from sixty-five years to their late nineties. They are predominantly female, representing the English working class and lower middle classes, with one or two exceptions. Many of the care assistants, who come from the nearby housing estate, are also representatives of the English working class. The ratio within the home of women to men is addressed within the study, as is the ratio of female to male carers. Furthermore, the issues of untrained, low-paid care workers are addressed, and how they impact on the daily practices of life in a residential nursing home in the modern era. All the data and analyses arise from the anthropologist's 'thick description' of the multi-faceted make-up of such an institution.

Anthropology at Home

During the year of fieldwork in the nursing home in rural Oxfordshire, a six-teen-mile drive from my home, I often experienced a sense of geographical isolation and distance from the community at large. Yes, I was doing anthro-pology at home and no, I did not have to learn another language or wear different clothes to those normally worn. However, a different 'language' was spoken by the employees and residents. Clothes that I wore were com-mented upon by residents and staff alike, whether it was 'Doc Marten boots' worn with a skirt, or black jacket and 'heels' worn for a funeral. In order to meet care assistants on their own ground, I would occasionally sit in the staff room, which was always thick with the 'smog' of cigarette smoke. Like Okely, I found that 'I unlearned my private school accent, changed clothing and body movements' (1996: 23) and could never get my demeanour quite right. On one occasion, a nephew of a wealthy resident could not believe that I was a law-abiding researcher, rather than some official 'checking up on her finances'. These finances were bequeathed to him in his aunt's will, which no doubt accounted for his sensitivity, but it made me realise that I did indeed look suspicious in that setting, no matter what I wore or how I spoke.

That many of the residents and staff became friends is seen not only in the descriptive chapters below, but also in the fact that they continued to expect me to visit the home, even in subsequent years. This in-depth period and the ensuing time are defined and described in the interpretation of the detailed patterns of life as found in the term 'thick description' attributed to Geertz (1973: 6) when describing the ethnography of an anthropologist:

> From one point of view, that of the textbook, doing ethnography is establishing rapport, selecting informants, transcribing texts, taking genealogies, mapping fields, keeping a diary and so on. But it is not these things that define the enter-prise. What defines it is the kind of intellectual effort it is: an elaborate venture in … 'thick description'.

Within the following chapters, we will see evidence of 'thick description', showing aspects of the view Geertz describes, for example how rapport was established with both residents and care assistants. Issues and ideas emerging in the course of the research are addressed according to various arguments in the literature on ageing, philosophy and the quality of life. I concentrate on the social and personal implications of dementia and its impact upon the quality of life for the resident as well as the employee. The use of ethnography and formulation from the Greek ἔ θνος ethnos, meaning 'folk, people or nation', and γράφω grapho, meaning 'writing', results in this description of the social discourse.

Subsequent chapters show the results of observations in the fieldwork, with one describing the care assistants at work with the residents; another detailing the case histories of people with dementia, and the social and behavioural aspects of their condition; and another emphasising the practicalities of social organisation within the nursing home, such as meal times and activities sessions. The discussion in the conclusion brings together the themes and ideas arising throughout, with regard to institutionalisation for both staff and residents, and the elusive theme of the 'quality of life', centring on routine and order within the notion of the institution as a 'home from home'.

If there is a culture within the nursing home itself, then this research endeavours to show the 'culture' wherever possible and where in particular it was enforced, both on residents and staff, especially with the manager's insistence on each individual classing it as their 'home from home'. Evidence of the use of the term 'home from home' in other parts of Europe is seen in the promotional literature for a large nursing home in Mallorca. The title of the information pack is 'Live as in your own home', inscribed in both Catalan and Spanish as early as the 1990s (Ministerio de Asuntos Sociales 1996). As will be seen here, the idea was not always a lived reality for the resident. The use of the word 'culture' here reflects the way in which it can be defined as referring to the care home's systems of values and accepted behaviour, often connected to one's social, regional or cultural heritage. In this context, it applies to a culture within institutions as well as the culture of the individual care home itself.

Both employees and residents as well as relatives were interested in the way that events within the social discourse of the nursing home would be written down. Relatives were quick to say how they hoped that memories of their family member would live on long after their death. This ethnography acknowledges my participation in the social discourse, as heard and observed, understood through participant observation and ultimately my ability to access and share in the ingredients, constituents and meaning of the discourse, both spoken and unspoken. This active participation is highlighted by the representation of the social discourse and social actions in the thumbnail sketches of 'thick description' as interpretation throughout the ethnography.

The many voices included here will show the anthropologist's assessment of the author's interpretation as being second-hand. However, as the study was that of 'anthropology at home', and as I was familiar with working in residential homes and au fait with the culture of nursing generally, I hope that the voices coming through are those of the residents and staff, and not only that of the researcher. The emphasis throughout the study is of it taking place within a nursing home, even in the areas where the most intimate tasks were undertaken, such as in bathrooms and bedrooms, and what took place there at any given time during the year, formed part of the social discourse and dialogue.

If the description is thick, this implies many and varied layers, which in turn represent voices, both of the people in the home and those associated with it: residents, carers, all manner of employees, managers, relatives and visitors. Within the voices interpreted here, the author's voice and her interpretation of how she heard those voices are present. Another deeper layer represents the observed, though unspoken layer, committed to paper as interpreted observations, written from the author's perceptions of what took place on a daily basis within the nursing home. That year, with its annual cycle of calendar events, such as the celebrations of Easter, Christmas and New Year, and the greeted onset of new seasons of spring and autumn, also revealed the dreaded onset of winter and its association with death. Moreover, those individual celebrations within the year, namely the birthdays of residents and staff, the acknowledgement of the deaths both of residents and their family members and staff, as well as the turnover of staff, including management, added to the intimate detail of everyday life as lived in the home.

Within the often unspoken nitty-gritty of my description lie even deeper issues, such as the confrontation of multiple losses: loss of spouse; loss of home; loss of friends; loss of pets; loss of possessions; loss of privacy; loss of identity; loss of good health; loss of way of life; and possible loss of a reason for living. These overall losses serve to inform the larger issue of the presence or lack of quality of life within the nursing home, both for the resident and the employee. Likewise, the gains found on moving into such an institution are described, as these too form some of the layers, all of which ultimately compose the larger picture, this culture; this experience of life and ultimate death.

As each chapter develops, the overall concerns of the quality of life within a care/nursing home are prioritised, such as privacy, the feminisation and the medicalisation of old age and the loss of independence, all addressed within the lived reality as portrayed. Other concerns that arise, such as boredom and the lack of choice, are considered with brief reference to philosophical works such as Foucault's 'On Power' (1988). Goffman's 1950s identification of 'total institution' is also reflected upon within the inherent need for members of society and their families to place relatives suffering from dementia and other illnesses in a 'safe' environment.

> The handling of many human needs by the bureaucratic organisation of whole blocks of people – whether or not this is a necessary or effective means of social organisation in the circumstances – is the key fact of total institutions. (Goffman 1961: 18)

In the 'total institution' described by Goffman, residents in a twenty-first-century institution such as a care home may find themselves in a place of controlled dependency and bureaucracy, which can in turn lead to helplessness. How this impacts on other residents who are lucid is also considered and the various reactions illustrated.

Foner's account of life in a residential nursing home in America in 1994, neatly entitled *The Caregiving Dilemma*, acknowledged that a nursing home life was equally that of the workers and their worlds as of the residents, revealing the institutional requirement for bureaucracy, resultant tensions and even the depersonalisation of staff. The following chapters stress how this occurs for patients in present-day long-term institutions. What is seen is a tendency, if not checked, for this to happen to staff in particular and also to residents. Depersonalisation results from the conflict between individuality and an invasive bureaucracy. When the institution itself is large, and when management is perceived to be both aloof and at a geographical distance, issues about the quality of life are at stake.

With its accent on the life experienced within the home, such an institution can inform our understanding of the social construction of old age and the treatment of frail older people well into the twenty-first century. This type of research resulting from oral narrative, case notes and discussions within the nursing home setting can inform staff, managers, families and residents, and may ultimately lead to an ideal of care for sick and frail older people. The emphasis on defining the group of residents as sick elderly people is central to residential living and its predictable institutional control. Within the following chapters, questions of independent or assisted living are addressed, while acknowledging the increasing immobility and cognitive decline of the residents.

The issue of marginalisation is encountered not only by the residents themselves but also by those who care for them, namely the low-earning, non-qualified women. The geographical location and isolation of the home, already mentioned, can contribute to marginalisation, especially when family members and friends, themselves older people, are unable to visit unless they have access to private transport. If such an institution is poorly served by public transport and if, as is evident, it is not surrounded by the usual societal infrastructure of shops, schools, churches, banks and public houses, the geographical isolation so easily results in marginalisation from society. For staff and management to get to work, all needed transport, though some carers were close enough to cycle in good weather. When this type of isolation is added to an already felt detachment such as the loneliness and the losses associated with old age, it becomes likely that emotions such as depression and dejection emerge. Rarely were exhilaration and joy observed, although there was always evidence of humour and laughter, however flippant. The encounter with death that both staff and residents face, often on a daily basis and always during that 'dreaded onset' of winter, may well account for the dependency on humour to deal with such sensitive and heart-felt concerns. The in-depth description used throughout will refer to these emotions, even though such subjective issues are not easy to describe.

Cicero, writing as Cato Major around 44 bc in his treatise *Cato Maior de Senectute*, 'On Old Age', was challenged by the retort, 'perhaps someone may reply that old age seems more tolerable to you because of your resources, means and social position' (Cicero 1923: 17). As wealth, and the accumulated wealth or the resource-rich ownership of one's own house in particular, is tied up with social position, then to be poor and old is a double bind, as compared to being old and financially secure. Add to this the loss of good health, and the double bind becomes a triple one of many and varied experiences of ageing. This is shown here in the narrative of *Living before Dying*, and the quality of a lived life within this residential home and its wider community, and as described in the poignant leitmotif, 'Imagining and Remembering Home'.

Chapter 1
THE SOCIAL AND BEHAVIOURAL IMPLICATIONS
OF PEOPLE WITH DEMENTIA

> Yesterday he tried to brush his teeth. Today he stared at the toothbrush as if to
> ask, What is this? One day he does a task but not the next.... I can now break
> tasks down into small step-by-step procedures. I get out both toothbrushes and
> put on paste while he watches. I hand him a brush and he imitates me.... When
> he can't do a task I try to accept it. But when he does it easily I make that a
> joyful occasion.
> —Murphey, *Day to Day*

Within the day-to-day working life of the home, all staff including cleaners,
maintenance men and kitchen staff mixed with people with dementia as
well as the other residents. It is the care assistants and nurses, however, who
have the most contact with the residents. As will be shown, there is little
or no formal training in becoming a care assistant, so the way one learns
depends on how one picks up skills and techniques while doing the job. It
also depends on how the nurse or senior care assistant imparts the necessary knowledge and skills. This is equally true when caring for people with
dementia in the nursing home and when caring for residents who are frail or
ill. It is more than possible that the care assistant with no training brings a set
of coping strategies to the job similar to that of a relative caring for a person
with dementia at home. These characteristics include patience, especially
when having to repeat oneself, kindness and humour. An important issue in
caring for someone with dementia is whether the carer, relative or employee
feels willing and able to do it, especially with the realisation of how demanding the job of caring becomes.

In the course of fieldwork, I increasingly encountered stories, narrated
by relatives of residents and written in the nursing and medical notes, of a
crisis or crises before admission to the nursing home. The one crisis that far
outnumbered other crises of admission due to illness and incapacity was that

of the onset and development of dementia and its associated physical and intellectual decline and confusion.

The early part of this chapter considers this particular diagnosis as reason for admission to the nursing home. Again and again, when looking at the coping strategies of families, there were limits as to what families could do for a relative with dementia in their endeavour to keep them safe and free from harm in their own home and community. The social dimensions of a relative with dementia are harsh and become almost impossible to live with, for example the constant wandering into busy streets, with neighbours, police or even caring members of the public bringing home the person with dementia at all times of the day or night; for a spouse, the sad awareness that the person they are now caring for is 'not the man/woman I married', added to the ever-present strain of carrying out all activities of daily living for their partner. On interviewing many people, it was clear that one of the most important parts of their life was the relationship of marriage. One of the coping strategies used by the partner of the ill spouse is that of distancing the present character of the ill husband or wife from that of the past, especially where aggressive behaviour becomes a dominant feature of the illness. Greater satisfaction from a lifelong loving relationship predicted the emergence of a coping strategy that allowed them to deal with the dependent relationship, at least before the onset of severe dementia. In this way, they were able to hang onto their good memories of the spouse and the marriage.

Dementia Elucidated

In interviewing caregivers as to the catalysts for moving relatives into institutions, namely nursing homes, Aneshensel et al. (1995: 199) found a number of reasons for admission. I shared my understanding and interpretation of these with the care assistants and nurses, who all agreed that these are comprehensive and accurate grounds for relatives seeking admission of their family member to residential care:

- too exhausted to carry on
- too difficult to lift and move the person
- person at risk of falling and injuring themselves
- loss of bowel and/or bladder control
- person became physically ill
- caregiver could not get help needed to care for the relative at home
- problem with behaviour, such as wandering or dangerous use of appliances
- person too aggressive to manage

- person no longer recognises family members
- caregiver became too ill to carry on

Most relatives and caregivers told of multiple reasons as catalysts for admission of their relatives to the care home. Here, the descriptive case studies of residents highlight the difficult and even embarrassing circumstances of dealing with dementia. The direct result of such occurrences on the family, main carer and neighbours in the community is also noted in terms of how each crisis eventually led to the need for residential care.

In the general understanding and parlance regarding dementia and Alzheimer's disease, a common definition is given as 'being out of one's mind'. The etymology of the word dementia comes from the Latin '*demens*', denoting members of society progressively and increasingly losing their mental capacity and the skills needed to carry out normal activities of everyday living (ADLs). Jonathan Miller, one-time president of the Alzheimer's Disease Society (ADS), is quoted as saying:

> Few illnesses are crueller than Alzheimer's disease. It clouds memory and obscures thought isolating people from the outside world. Books and newspapers are impossible to decode, ordinary conversation sounds like meaningless babble, friends and family become strangers. (Miller 1998)

From this description, one can see what a profound effect the disease has, not only on the person with dementia but also on the carer, husband/wife, son/daughter-in-law, niece/nephew, grandchildren and so on. The most daunting aspect of dementia is that it is 'a progressive failure of most cerebral functions' (Jacques 1992: 1) and, at present, medically irreversible. Some people with dementia are also found to have symptoms of depression, visual and auditory hallucinations and delusions of theft or persecution. Other changes in a person's behaviour include wandering, day/night reversal, aggression, altered eating habits such as binge eating, faecal and urinary incontinence, lack of sexual inhibition and increased vulnerability. The terms 'dementia' and 'Alzheimer's disease' are often used interchangeably. Most of the symptoms currently recognised as pertaining to Alzheimer's disease were identified in an original study by Alois Alzheimer, the German neuro-physicist after whom the disease was named (Alzheimer 1907). The early signs of Alzheimer's disease, although varying from individual to individual, include most or all of the following:

- short-term memory loss
- repeating conversations
- anxiety in making decisions

- difficulty in grasping new ideas or adapting to change
- lack of concern about other people such as family members and family events

In addition to these signs, there are often problems with speech, both understanding and being understood, a lack of bodily coordination and failure to recognise objects even though the eyesight is not impaired.

As the condition worsens, there occurs great loss of practical skills such as cooking, the ability to tell the time, washing and dressing or maintaining personal hygiene. This progressive deterioration is noted in the case histories in this chapter, showing how they contributed to a collection of crises in caring for people with dementia, sometimes known as the disease burden.

The Alzheimer's Disease Society (ADS) estimates that dementia currently affects over 850,000 people in the UK: one in twenty people aged over sixty-five and one in five people aged over eighty are affected (Alzheimer's Disease Society 2014). The Society's submission to the Royal Commission on Long-Term Care stated their belief that talk of 'a demographic time bomb' (in the media for instance) was misleading, in that it would be a steady growth in dementia predicted over the next twenty-five years, not a dramatic one. In highlighting this to the Royal Commission, they reiterated their belief that the state can provide for people's needs as they age, and that rather than being defined as a burden, they say 'that a sustainable system can be developed' to meet those needs (Alzheimer's Disease Society 1998). Papastavrou et al. (2007) importantly showed how relatives acting as carers developed coping strategies in their endeavours to reduce their load as caregiver and ultimately become better able to manage caregiving complexities, aggression both verbal and physical being the most difficult to face.

Within the nursing home itself, the term 'dementia' was used consistently when staff described people with Alzheimer's disease as well as residents with other forms of dementia. Apart from where medical diagnosis of Alzheimer's disease is given, the term 'dementia' will be used throughout this chapter. Out of twenty-nine residents in one wing of the home, sixteen were admitted due to diagnosis of dementia of considerable severity. Two other women had long-term histories of schizophrenia, and one other woman suffered from paranoia. Of the remaining residents, eight were admitted due to a decline in physical health, especially following debilitating strokes; one woman had been in an institution since her youth and another with gross physical deformities had been hospitalised in a psychiatric unit since her teens. On another wing, fourteen out of twenty-four residents had varying degrees of dementia, while on the remaining wing there were thirteen people with dementia out of a total of twenty-two. Of the other nine residents, one was a long-term schizophrenic. This totalled forty-three people with dementia to be cared for 24/7. What these numbers represent, including those people with schizophrenia, is a high incidence of residents with disorders for which the carers, both care assistants and nurses, have little or no training. Often the family caring for them at home had insufficient understanding about what was happening to their relative, with occasional or scant professional support, as well as experiencing the stigma associated with dementia. The care assistants in the nursing home each had their own way of working with people with dementia, representing personal coping strategies, some more experienced and sympathetic than others.

This chapter will show from case histories, gleaned from nursing care notes, medical notes and relatives' narratives where possible, how certain behaviour becomes difficult to cope within the domestic situation and the community. Observations of the crisis situations and challenging behaviour encountered in the patients with dementia form part of the findings presented in this chapter. This behaviour associated with dementia becomes so difficult for the carer and so potentially harmful for the sufferer that admission to institutional care proves to be the only solution for some people and their families. Care in the community, as well as use of the few day care centres available, has been tried and severely tested, as well as continuous care by relatives. However, when these situations present themselves, they usually do so as a crisis to the social and medical services, which then in turn prioritise according to need. There was a growing awareness among the carers and staff at the nursing home that these particular crises in dementia are being prioritised, resulting in more people with dementia being admitted than in the past. Within this general feeling and understanding is the growing awareness that the workload associated with these admissions is becoming 'heavier'. During the fieldwork, I endeavoured to look at what this meant for the staff, as well as what it meant in 'lived' terms for relatives or neighbours involved in caring, and show from various accounts, case studies and incidents how the quality of life, in all cases, was in question. This concerns the quality of working life for the employee as well as the quality of life generally for the resident and the family. Each person in the case history is named by fictitious first name only, but the content of the narrative pertains to one person and one extended family alone.

Dementia as Evolving Crises

Doreen

Doreen, a seventy-four-year-old woman who was widowed just after the war, later married and divorced, was admitted from her own home in a nearby town, and had been resident in the nursing home for two years at the time of the study. Her next of kin is a male second cousin who with his wife lived in the same market town.

The personal profile written in her nursing care notes shows that she was born and brought up in the Oxfordshire town that remained her home until nursing home admission. She was an only child, and sadly her first husband was killed in a flying accident at the end of the Second World War. During the war, she worked in the local depot as supplies supervisor and then spent a period in Germany after the war. She was in employment all her life, retiring as a bookmaker. Her father died of a brain haemorrhage in 1968, aged seventy-two, while her mother lived to age ninety-one, dying in 1986, when Doreen was already in her sixties and living in the family home. She used to play the piano, read novels and enjoyed dancing.

Her medical notes start before 1950, showing a continuity of care within the National Health Service, then in its early stages. She had always been a fit woman but was diagnosed as having cervical spondylosis when aged fifty-two and Alzheimer's disease at aged sixty-nine. As with many of the residents in the study diagnosed with Alzheimer's disease, Doreen was referred by her GP to the psycho-geriatric services who on examining her found her to be extremely well physically. However, her mental state was found to be poor, the specialist noting a score of 3/10 for her cognitive function tests. It was established that the only word she could say with certainty was her name. The severity of her long-term and short-term memory loss was such that her ability to keep her house clean, as well as care for her own needs, had deteriorated greatly. As with so many of the residents suffering from dementia, she presented as a crisis. The crisis, in fact, was an extreme emergency. She had found her elderly gentleman lodger on the kitchen floor, dying. When she found him, she was not aware of the reality of the situation and it was only when her cousin called at the house that the situation became apparent. It was also established after he had been admitted to hospital that the lodger had inadvertently, or possibly knowingly, managed to conceal the severity of her disability through constant prompts and supervision while he lived there. It became rapidly obvious that Doreen was incapable of caring for herself. Two weeks prior to this emergency, she had driven her car with no apparent comprehension of the severity of her disability without any trouble on the road. She had lived with her mother, in this same house, and had been born there, so was completely at ease and familiar with her surroundings.

When the psycho-geriatrician visited her at home after the emergency, Doreen presented as dishevelled, grubby and bemused, with neither a grasp of who the doctor was nor why she had let him into her home, which was alarming in itself for her personal safety. The house was described as having an overwhelming smell of cat faeces, with cat food and cat faeces scattered around. The refrigerator smelt of sour milk and other stale food items, which had clearly been there for many weeks. The geriatrician arranged urgent referral to social services. Meanwhile, the battery in her car was dismantled and as she had driven the car only recently, the DVLA were duly informed by her cousin for an immediate ban on her driving.

Following this crisis, the family involvement of her cousin and his wife was such that they would help her wash and dress at weekends and provide midday meals. The cousin went in daily to get her tea at 5 p.m., while one or both got her ready for bed at 7–8 p.m. They were mostly concerned about her isolation and poor quality of life, as she spent much time alone. She repeatedly talked to herself, not usually understandable to others, but showed an enjoyment of company. She was also noticeably frightened by loud noises. The cousin was also troubled about faeces in the sink in the bathroom, possible smearing and deteriorating toilet habits. Due to all these factors, respite care was arranged and Doreen was admitted to residential care for some weeks. The desired plan for her future safety, which all parties were in agreement with (presumably except Doreen herself, with little self-awareness and knowledge), was for admission to long-term residential care as soon as possible. However, as can be seen from the summary below, this took more than three years. The reality of those three years, both for her and the relatives and carers, was one of constant worry and concern, especially at night when there was no active support system for her alone at home. Meanwhile, her main carers were invited to meetings of a carers' group, and home care started, which consisted of washing and dressing her every day and providing lunch twice a week. Over the years, these care assistants saw a gradual deterioration. A 'sitting' service, whereby a carer would visit twice a week and stay one and a half hours, was provided. One of the problems encountered when she was eventually offered a place at a day care unit was her tendency to wander far from the observant care of the day care assistants, who were not able to give her one-to-one attention.

The following summary shows the type of community care and support offered and made available to the patient and her family after the crisis was first observed. In her early seventies, home care was provided on weekdays at midday. Some months later, Doreen refused respite care, and the following year refused day care. By the end of the summer of the same year, a community psychiatric nurse began to visit Doreen at home. A year later, Doreen began attending a day centre one day a week, and the following year this was increased to two days a week. During this time, Doreen was admitted for respite care one week in every six. Three years after care began, recommendation was made for an additional day at the centre and an increase of respite care to one in every four weeks; an application was made for permanent residential care and her cousin was granted power of attorney. Four long years after community care began, Doreen was accepted for admission to the care home and appeared to settle well into residential accommodation.

Having been diagnosed as suffering from dementia four years prior to admission, relatives and carers said that the advancement of the illness became more noticeable in the six months prior to admission.

On meeting Doreen in the nursing home, she presented as capable, mobile and smartly turned out, which masks her limitations. In my first meeting with her, I observed her talking fairly loudly and with animation to 'Susee', her reflection in the mirror. The notes in her care plan (written by one of the nurses) say that she repeats key phrases but is never known to express herself with lucidity. Also noted is that 'she seems to have a pleasant state of mind' and always seemed content. What this value appraisal meant was never fully explained to me, but on observing Doreen and working alongside the care assistant who looked after her, Doreen always appeared smiling and content. Her nursing care notes mention that although Doreen has expressive dysphasia, which is deficiency in speech generation and comprehension, she can be understood if the listener picks up certain words that she uses. As mentioned above, she will stand in front of a mirror and talk coherently to her reflection, but cannot be understood face to face in conversation. Doreen's care notes state that she mixes well with other residents, which is something I observed in her, even though she did not hold a conversation. Although we were never able to hold a conversation together, she would always greet me with a smile and try to communicate with words I could not understand. She repeated many routines – for example, when out in the garden, she tended to walk around the flowerbed again and again. This 'wandering', highlighted in her care plan, is often presented as a problem when looking after people with dementia. Kelly (1993: 3) says wandering can take the form of 'aimless restless pacing, or of searching and seeking behaviour'. In a review of the literature, Lin Gu says that 'there is lack of a systematic management strategy to manage the wandering of people with dementia' (Lin Gu 2015: 456). However, as Doreen did not present with aimless pacing, even when regularly walking around the flowerbeds, a management strategy did not appear to be needed. Her cousin stressed that in the crisis leading up to her admission, the state of her house, especially the presence of cat faeces and her own defecation in inappropriate places, was most distressing. He and his family had been deeply concerned about the fact that she could so easily have 'wandered off' and eventually come to harm. As next of kin, and including his wife and adult daughter, he stressed how extremely relieved and delighted they were to have their relative admitted to the nursing home.

Life for Doreen in the nursing home involved the care assistant attending to her personal needs, such as washing and dressing, which she was unable to do herself. Doreen had some beautiful clothes and always looked well presented. Her walk was of someone who took pride in how she looked. Although she did not appear to speak coherently, she seemed to respond well to the care assistant washing and dressing her. The most noticeable lack of coordination occurred when putting her shoes on, which could only be achieved with some pressure, thereby causing discomfort. She had lost the ability to put her clothes or shoes on herself, but could protest if discomfort was felt. The hairdresser employed in the nursing home kept Doreen's hair nicely cut and set, with the overall impression of someone well turned out.

What is most evident about Doreen within this study is that her presence was often only noticed by her quietness, not necessarily silence but her lack of verbal communication. She responded quietly and warmly when touched on her arm, for example, and with response in her eyes when hearing something she understood and could identify with. There was definite evidence of recognition and response to her main care assistant when she explained to Doreen that she was moving to another job. She then had to start to trust her new carer, something I could only begin to observe as the research was near completion. Although quiet, she was not a solitary person, as evident in her incoherent chatter and a regular seeking out of one or two of the men sitting in the shared lounge.

Amy

Amy was another resident diagnosed with dementia. Prior to her admission into residential care, her recent years represented much loneliness and loss of identity. Eighty-six years old, Amy moved to Oxfordshire nine years before moving to the nursing home. This was in order to live near her son, but she had never settled and regretted the move bitterly. Amy was born and brought up in a Yorkshire town and lived all her life there until widowhood. She was happily married to a local businessman and was an extremely active woman. Even after her move south, she walked miles every day into town, where she would eat her lunch in a cafe as she did not enjoy cooking. She failed to make any real friends or acquaintances during the nine years since moving south. She had one son and a daughter-in-law. Her son, to whom she was devoted, worked overseas, but she described her daughter-in-law as a 'hard woman' even though she regularly visited her in the nursing home. As the son often worked abroad, responsibility for Amy had fallen on the daughter-in-law, who was in full-time work and therefore felt that she could not manage.

Amy had been partially deaf since the age of fifty, had degenerative disease of her joints and had fallen and fractured her ankle. She was referred to the Community Psychiatric Nurse (CPN) after the fracture, as she was becoming more forgetful and her family worried about her being alone. According to the CPN, this move to the south of England was deeply felt. Two brothers and a younger sister were still living in Sheffield, and there was no history of mental illness in the family. She had a history of alcoholism and one admission to a local health unit in a confused state, with a possible intake of one bottle of whisky and one bottle of sherry every two days. She was diagnosed as having chronic cognitive impairment, depression and the results of chronic alcohol intoxication, which were impossible to separate in the diagnosis. She was transferred to a local psychiatric hospital and then discharged to the nursing home.

During the study, I did not meet any of Amy's family and in my field notes she is characterised by her silence and quiet manner. She was well liked by the staff who cared for her but was not often included in activities by the occupational activities person, as those activities centred around the more vocal and lucid residents. When during an activities session she was shown books with photographs of Oxfordshire at the turn of the century, she naturally did not recognise places as did the residents born locally, but enjoyed looking at the photos of buildings, canals and transport reminiscent of her own locality. She was animated, pointing and smiling at the pictures so similar to those seen by her in the north of England in her childhood and youth. I return to this idea of reminiscence later in this chapter and also describe the activity session using the photographs in Chapter 4.

To this end, the aim of Amy's care plan was for her to remain in a safe environment and to be free from any possible danger. Her care notes said little about her, only that 'Amy is a quiet woman with a warm smile', and nothing of a social profile. What was stated in her care plan, though, was the need for supervision when washing herself and especially that she was prone to 'wander and confusion'. Amy did not represent a 'heavy workload' to the care assistants like other people with cognitive decline, especially some of the men, but she showed little interaction and response, and certainly no conversation. This in itself meant that the care assistant or nurse often had to interpret her needs and wants, usually by a process of elimination, which on most occasions worked well but could be emotionally draining.

Gwyneth

Gwyneth had moved to the nursing home two years before the study started, having been admitted from a nearby town, where her son and daughter lived. In her late seventies and widowed for six years, her family felt that her life had lacked continuity of late. She tended to be confused about time and place and, like a few other residents, needed to be reassured that money was not necessary as most things in the home were provided for, and few if any residents carried money on them. She liked watching the television and enjoyed company. Her cat was brought to the home with her and became the nursing home's cat. Having been diagnosed with dementia as her reason for admission to the home, Gwyneth was seen to sometimes wander at night, predominantly suffering from short-term memory loss.

Her medical notes showed many entries and referrals during the 1960s, when she was described as 'anorexic', with the eventual diagnosis of anxiety depressive state being made in the local psychiatric hospital. This was an exacerbation of a personality disorder but she also had a surgical abortion, as she was diagnosed as being at risk of a miscarriage. As the climate surrounding such procedures was one of near secrecy, it is more than possible that this disturbed her mental well-being, as shown in her later state of anxiety and depression. She was diagnosed with epilepsy in mid-life, and later had surgery for cancer of the bowel. When in her early seventies, dementia was diagnosed. She was referred to a gerontologist who found her cognitive test scores to be poor. A social report was made, during which assessment her daughter had the opportunity to voice her concerns about her mother. She was well supported by her family of one daughter and two sons, whom the social worker mentioned as having considerable obligations between them. It was stated in the social assessment that these obligations came into conflict with each other at times of high stress, and although all her family cared and looked after her, no one household could take her in, resulting in increased stress for all. Gwyneth's increasing frailty and dependency was noted by others, including neighbours and friends, and a burglary in her house resulted in considerable damage, not only to property but also to her confidence; she was seriously shaken. Her cognitive impairment interfered with her ability to cook safely or systematically, and she burnt or undercooked food. At night, she regularly left the house and often found it difficult to make her own way home. The psycho-geriatrician reported: 'By averages I feel she will fall foul of unsympathetic people'. Gwyneth herself stated that she wanted to be looked after, so day care was offered until the permanent environment of the nursing home was found. All present at the assessment believed it necessary for the power of attorney to be given. She had a wait of less than two years before being admitted to the nursing home.

A number of the care plans written out for the residents were brief, containing minimal information or advice as to what the main needs of the person were. This was the case for Gwyneth, whose main needs, well known to the care assistants looking after her, were for assistance in aspects of daily living. She was unable to attend to her own hygiene needs, such as washing, brushing her teeth or brushing her hair, and only walked independently with encouragement. This meant that when staff members were busy, she was taken in a wheelchair for such activities as hairdressing and meal times, whereas in fact she could walk. She needed assistance to the toilet, and a mechanical ambulift was necessary for use by the care assistants to put her in a bath. Gwyneth also had a history of falls, which could well account for the care assistants using the wheelchair rather than encouraging her to walk. Like Doreen, it was difficult to understand what Gwyneth said, although she was happy to have someone sit and listen to her, endeavouring to answer in all the right places.

Matilda

A local Oxfordshire woman, Matilda, in her late eighties, was admitted from a community hospital a year prior to the study. She had been widowed for six years and had suffered mild depression for ten years, which took the form of agitation and anxiety. The crisis for admission had been precipitated by a fractured pelvis and anaemia. There was evidence of self-neglect and deterioration in general health, which necessitated long-term care.

Her medical notes read as a well-documented history of depression and psychiatric assistance. A written history showed that she had been referred to the CPN in her seventies, when first treated with medication for a depressive illness, whereupon her depression lifted, though not totally. Prior to nursing home admission, the CPN and the district nursing service noted a decreased appetite, weight loss and loss of self-caring skills, such as dressing herself. Her son and daughter related that she was not eating well, not cooking and failing in her self-care. A 'meals on wheels' service was offered and subsequently cancelled as she did not eat any of the food, regularly throwing the meals away. Matilda had faecal incontinence and refused any help from her son. Her diagnosis was of a depressive illness with cognitive decline, most probably dementia.

She presented with her crisis of admission following a hospital admission due to a fractured pelvis, whereupon she was visited by the community psychiatric team, as ward nurses were concerned over her poor fluid intake. During her admission to a district community hospital, her GP wrote to social services, pointing out that three years ago he had written mentioning that a nursing home would be 'the best protection for her', but that others did not share his view. The GP had noted the excellent support from her family when she had continued to live alone in her caravan, probably masking her true need for long-term care, and within a few months she was admitted to the nursing home.

Her care plan, with sparse details and no social profile entered, stated that she was unable to wash herself and therefore needed assistance, whereas in reality she would often only need reminding. She achieved all other aspects of daily living herself, such as walking to the dining area for meals. In all respects of living, she was seen as one of the 'lighter' people in the workload but at times was found to be non-communicative and therefore 'not easy' to care for. She shared a room and both residents sat in it all day rather than use the communal lounge. Staff members were informed by relatives that because of previous self-isolation, including living in a mobile home due to penury before she was widowed, she did not enjoy the company of large numbers of people. She was a very quiet woman but enjoyed talking about her family when prompted. Her symptoms were more of depression than dementia; as mentioned earlier, depression often occurs in people with dementia. Both depression and dementia are clinically significant. What this meant in reality for Gwyneth was that she could sometimes be enjoined in conversation, especially if one was aware of her biography and made memory prompts. However, there was a sadness in this woman that can only be described as the *loneliness of dementia*, which I pick up in the next case history.

Lilian

Lilian, often described as a 'character' by family and friends, and aged in her nineties, was admitted during the early part of the study from her daughter's home in the same county. Her granddaughter worked and lived locally. Lilian had been widowed at least twenty years before admission. She recovered from scarlet fever when a child and a hysterectomy in her late forties, so could be seen to be a survivor. In her medical notes, there is a fairly well-documented psycho-geriatric history. She had lived with her married daughter for twenty years but began to think that she was only there for a holiday, telling people she would return to Birmingham. She became more and more confused and disoriented, with poor hearing and cognitive decline. Her self-care skills declined and although she fed and dressed herself, a nurse came to her home once a week to wash her. She was not incontinent but frequently had faeces stains in her underpants, probably because she was unable to clean herself. She was described by a visitor from the psychiatric service as being rather lonely during the day, living a fairly separate life from the daughter and son-in-law, spending most of her time in her room with an unread newspaper in her lap. Once a month she attended a women's guild and was said to greatly enjoy it. Lunches were arranged for her at the local Alzheimer's club.

Overall, she was fit and well physically. An entry in her GP notes stated that there was no past psychiatric history, but a family note describing her 'profile' mentions postnatal depression after the birth of her only child. Born and brought up in Birmingham with 'a content although poor childhood', her family and friends described her as a happy and confident person. Lilian was found to be very bright at school, but as there was little money she had to leave, despite being offered a scholarship. Upon leaving school, she worked at the Post Office and eventually became a chief wages clerk. She also had an extra job as an invigilator at examinations, married a civil servant and had a happy marriage until her husband died when they were both in their seventies. Her family were still keen to look after her with the involvement of a day centre run by social services. Her only sister, aged eighty-nine, lived fifty miles away in another county.

Lilian's situation and condition was reviewed a year after initial community psychiatric service involvement, due to deterioration and vivid hallucinations, and a month later she was interviewed by an associate specialist in psychiatry. She was found on examination to be appropriately dressed and extremely cheerful. However, it was noted that she appeared to laugh during much of the examination with no reference to what was actually happening. She did become a little more serious on not knowing the meaning of some of the questions, even somewhat irritable about them. She was described as 'very confused' and even had difficulty recognising her daughter. The problems presenting were those of getting up in the night, wandering around the house, and sometimes starting to dress at 4 a.m. (day/night reversal). She was unable to clean herself after using the lavatory. She apparently could not eat in a 'proper' fashion and was unable to ask verbally for anything. Lilian was said to just point at her clothes and her bed when ready to dress or go to bed. The diagnosis made was of severe dementia with a recent history of transient ischaemic attack (mini-stroke).

In the care home, Lilian would rarely talk, would sit quietly and was fully capable of walking from her room to the main lounge. At times, she was observed to be angry, shouting and upset, more often than not because she was being asked to do something she did not understand. There were times when she recognised family members who visited, but mostly she had an air of loneliness about her and even when sitting near other people there was a profound sense of her 'being alone'.

What all these women have in common is their loss of verbal communication skills. This could well impact on why they were so 'silent' in the study, whereas men like Bob and Arthur, described in the following case histories, appeared again and again. Even their written care plans were fuller, proactive and descriptive. Men such as Bob and Arthur had lost many of their skills of verbal communication also, but relatives' accounts of their pre-illness personalities indicated assertiveness of character over and beyond assertiveness of verbal communication skills and even aggression. In the introduction to *Perceiving Women*, Shirley Ardener (1975: xii) acknowledged Charlotte Hardman's original use of the term 'muted group', which the Ardeners then proposed as a theory whereby dominant modes of expression in any society … [are] generated by the dominant structures within it as defined by Edwin Ardener (1975: 22). They stated that 'it does not require that the muted be actually silent [but] the important issue is whether they are able to say all that they would wish to say, where and when they wish to say it' (Ardener 1993: 7–8). What I term 'mutedness' here can be understood as a development of this muted group theory. Where anthropologists and others were encouraged to give more attention to forms of communication and modes of expression that might be missed, my thinking on 'mutedness' stems from the use of the mute in music. Taking the trombone as an example, when a mute is used, the sound of the instrument is never fully silenced, rather it is quietened and muted, reducing the volume and, therefore, its power. Following on from 'muted group theory', use of the term 'mutedness' can be useful here in illustrating certain controlling behaviour towards older people, including that of infantilisation.

Is it possible then that the women with dementia highlighted in the case studies were 'muted' in their lives prior to the onset of dementia, and that the ensuing loss of verbal skills in communication only further extends their mutedness? The theory of muting is not just concerned with oral conversation, as language is not the only way of communicating. Sometimes the very seating arrangements in a lounge could inhibit communication, if a resident was unable to attract the attention of staff for example. Therefore, for women residents in the nursing home, including those not ill with dementia, inarticulateness and lack of persuasion in getting their demands or needs met may be accentuated in the presence of other residents and inhibited by the men in particular, who often find more aggressive ways of articulating their need for attention. The next two case studies describe two of the male residents.

Dementia and Masculinity

Arthur, aged eighty-seven, had lived at the nursing home for two years at the time of the study. His adopted daughter lived locally, while his wife lived in a different nursing home. He had lived in his rented home for fifty years, and modernisation of it had been refused, either by him or by his landlord. There was no running water, only an outside bathroom and toilet, and the house was in a poor state of repair. Since being in the nursing home, Arthur had

had no contact with his wife, and his daughter visited only occasionally. In the home, he enjoyed talking about his time in the army and abroad during the war, although staff mentioned that they thought he had a tendency to fabricate. Although he talked to residents and staff, he never got involved with group activities, possibly due to a poor concentration span. If he left the home unsupervised, he would easily make his way to the city sixteen miles away, being able to follow road signs. His Jack Russell dog had died two years earlier, and he still reminisced about her, in fact mentioning her more often than his wife.

His dementia was first noted ten years prior to nursing home admission, whereupon his wife was moved to a council flat for her own safety, due to his increasing aggression towards her. Arthur was self-neglecting, dangerous in the house, leaving the gas on and burning pans after forgetting them. He consistently refused home care and by the time of admission to the nursing home he had become extremely disoriented. Of his mental ability and comprehension, it was noted that he understood what was said and responded well.

In his medical notes, his home and his GP were recorded as being in the city of Oxford and at age thirty-five his occupation was that of welder. Nearly thirty years later, a hospital letter noted that the car factory was his place of work. A social worker had been involved after social problems presented at home. Later, the daughter brought to attention the less than adequate housing conditions and unsatisfactory marital relationship of the parents. There had been no repairs to the house since it was built eighty years ago, with no inside toilet, no running hot water and no bathroom. As the Environmental Health Department stated that the house was not fit to live in, the housing application to rehouse his wife was successful and a warden-controlled flat offered to her was eagerly accepted.

What follows is a summarised series of events, well documented in his medical notes, which showed an 'evolving crisis' and what that meant to his immediate neighbours in the street in which he lived. This is a good, if extreme example of what crises in people with dementia present in the months and years leading up to admission to residential care. This account will also show how long it took for a solution to the crisis to be found.

Ten years prior to admission, a neighbour wrote to Arthur's doctor showing concern for his safety (and for his wife's safety until she moved out). The neighbour described their row of terraced houses and of her being out at work all day and how worried she was about a fire risk from her neighbour, Arthur. This was because she knew that Arthur would often light the gas stove, sit down and doze, wake and decide to go to the pub for lunch, leaving the gas burning. The doctor answered by saying that although he could understand her fears, Arthur would not accept advice or therapy and could not be forced to do so unless he became mentally certifiable or a serious public health risk. The GP added that he had never sectioned a patient within his practice under the Mental Health Act.

Four years passed, and after growing concern for Arthur's living conditions, with his increasing inability to manage living alone, his GP requested a visit from a psycho-geriatrician, but Arthur refused to be seen. Two months later, the psycho-geriatrician gained entry via a home care assistant who happened to be visiting at the same time. It was noted that there had been a long history of cognitive decline, with increased dependence, self-neglect, disorientation and wandering. The pressing concerns were the long walks and cycle rides Arthur was taking, during which he became lost. A significant problem was Arthur's own safety in operating his cooker, as he had a history of burning saucepans. He was observed to be dishevelled and unwashed and, though coherent, rambling in speech. There was no evidence of depression or abnormal perceptions but his mini-mental state cognitive examination revealed a low score, showing poor orientation and poor short-term memory. He was also noted to show no insight into his problems. Recommendations were made for a social worker to liaise with the city's social services and find out who should be organising home assessments and preventing mishaps with the cooker. As his diagnosed dementia was likely to progress, it was deemed appropriate to seek the involvement of the community psychiatry service. There was to be an assessment centre meeting with the home care organiser and Arthur's daughter, at his home. Other problems observed were leaving the front door open when there were large amounts of money in the house, poor personal hygiene and the refusal of an offer for someone to do his laundry. He showed signs of poor nutrition, often leaving 'meals on wheels' untouched. It was therefore necessary to increase support, for example for home care to attend twice a day to do a basic safety check on devices, such as the bottled gas for his cooker. His usual home care visits were to increase to three times a day to include extra help washing clothes and shopping for nutritious food. A district nurse based at a doctor's surgery and the community resource team for the promotion of mental health in elderly people were to be contacted and he was to have much-needed help in sorting out his finances.

Six months later, there was increasing concern for his progressive deterioration noted by all parties involved, and he was seen by a consultant in old age psychiatry. His mini-mental state score had dropped compared with that from six months previously. The difficulty in self-care was seen to be more severe, representing a decline. The essential problem was that of social care, as evidenced by rotting food in the kitchen. This was complicated by his relative lack of insight and rather authoritarian pre-morbid personality, which meant he was unwilling to admit difficulties. He did agree to more intensive help from home care, which involved visits three times a day by the home care services. The psycho-geriatrician anticipated further intellectual decline over the months ahead and foresaw the ultimate need for admission to residential care. It was also anticipated that it would become easier for Arthur to accept more help as his decline continued.

Another eight months passed, whereupon the GP wrote to social services mentioning the distress and anxiety from three of Arthur's neighbours concerning his condition.

Seven years later, the same neighbour wrote directly to social services, with a copy to Arthur's GP. The neighbour reported an incident she had encountered on returning home from work, when she found Arthur trapped in his front window. It seemed he must have locked himself out (which he did daily) and was attempting to get back in via the front window, which in the absence of cords, fell on his back. He was too frightened to go backwards or forwards and was totally confused. With only elderly neighbours to help, it was difficult to move him. The neighbour wrote of more typical incidents such as the gas cooker being left on, burning pans and Arthur's forgetfulness about his gas fire being switched on in his front room. She was very concerned about the fire risk to all their properties from burned saucepans on Arthur's stove.

A month after this incident, a Court Protection Order was filed with an accompanying certificate of incapacity. Arthur was then admitted to the nursing home.

What this account represents is seven years of intense living, both for Arthur and his neighbours, during which he seemed near to danger and his neighbours despaired of the risks incurred by his living conditions. These seven years condensed here into a few pages of description represent, for the neighbours, long years in their concern and anxieties for his and their safety. Obviously, they were concerned as well for the security of their own properties but what mostly came across from the written accounts was genuine neighbourly interest and concern. In other instances described in this chapter, families did not have to wait so long for admission to residential care. At times, the liaison between social services and GPs is not as prompt as it could be. When the community psycho-geriatric teams become involved, swifter outcomes such as admission to residential care are usually achieved.

Arthur's care plan in the nursing home was carefully worked out, showing a number of areas classed as problems, namely short-term memory loss. Included in this was his fluctuating mood, along with aggression, and his constant wandering out of the grounds. He was said to be disoriented as to time and place, frighteningly so, to the extent that he entered other residents' rooms, collecting their belongings. The aim, therefore, guided by his care plan, was for Arthur to be calm and at ease in his surroundings and for him to accept that he was living in a residential home. Within the care plan was the aim that other residents' belongings remain in place in their rooms and that the residents be free from the worry of someone entering their room. Senior care assistants with an understanding of people with dementia informed me that wandering is one of the most problematic aspects of dementia to handle because it is difficult to stop and there is no respect for the personal space of others. The care associated with this problem entailed reminding Arthur as necessary about events, time and place. He would not go into rooms when firmly told that this was a 'ladies' room'. A minimal approach to care was suggested for when he was aggressive, but he soon forgot this behaviour and would accept care later. If he wandered out of the grounds, it was noted that he would always come back by car, if offered a lift.

Another problem attributed to his short-term memory loss was his inability to maintain an adequate standard of hygiene and dress. If left to his own devices, he would dress inappropriately, for example by putting his clothes on inside out and back to front, and refuse to wash. The aim, as written in his care plan, was for him to receive an adequate standard of hygiene and dress, and the care pattern was of encouragement to do things for himself. It was noted that Arthur did not like a direct approach but that all procedures could and should be explained to him. This included trying to bath Arthur once a week or when necessary, if soiled. A related problem was that of urinary and faecal incontinence and inappropriate depositing of faeces. In effect, this meant he was at pains to hide the faeces. Thus, the aim of everyone caring for Arthur was that he be continent where possible, which involved reminding him at regular intervals as to the location of the lavatory. He would use the WC and occasionally ask for directions to it, greatly objecting to wearing pads and always removing them if one was put on him. The care plan reminded care assistants and nurses to regularly check his room for hidden faeces. Observation and discussion of how difficult this was for the care assistants regularly features throughout this study.

During the first formal review of his care plan, concern was voiced about the level of physical aggression and his constant wandering out of grounds. Wandering was risky as the driveway of the home led directly onto a road with a fifty mile an hour speed limit. It was suggested that the home manager write to social services to endeavour to get extra funding for one-to-one care from 1 p.m. to 6 p.m. daily. Unfortunately, social services were not able to meet the financial demands for this type of care and, at times, Arthur often only had slippers on his feet, not shoes, in the hope that he would not walk far from the security of the nursing home. To be seen walking in slippers on the main road near the home would be an indication to a sympathetic person driving or walking by that Arthur was not in the place he was expected to be in. On a number of occasions, he was encouraged to walk back to the nursing home by a concerned driver or pedestrian.

As mentioned, Arthur's care plan was explicit and a reasonable guide for care assistants, both experienced and not so experienced. The high level of attention that he needed was evidenced by the way in which his care plan was written up, especially bearing in mind that he could become aggressive. However, what is interesting is the kind of input and effort put into the plan on behalf of a health professional, namely the nurse. As was pointed out earlier, when looking at the case histories of the women, their care plans were often scanty, making minimal reference even to their biographies. Not so with Arthur, and equally not so with Bob, as now described.

Bob

A retired butcher, eighty-eight-year-old Bob had been in the nursing home for four years at the time of the study. His wife was still alive and living in their marital home. He was admitted from a hospital assessment centre following worsening aggression towards his wife. He was diagnosed with senile dementia three years prior to admission and his slow slide into dementia made it very difficult for his wife to care for him. He used to lock his wife out of the house and not allow visitors in, at times becoming physically aggressive towards her. She put a lock on the phone to prevent him phoning his doctor continually to say he was ill. His wife was highly practical, asking for day care, more for his stimulation than for her sake. He attended a day care centre three times weekly while his wife attended the relative support group, and Bob was referred to the community psychiatric nursing service for support at home.

As with some of the case histories mentioned above, here follows a summary of events that led up to Bob's admission to residential care. This in turn shows a pattern in the emerging social crises as presented in all these accounts.

Ten years prior to admission, Bob had bilateral cataract extraction, which with spectacles achieved good vision in both eyes. At a similar time, he attended a pain relief unit due to a long history of non-specific pain. No relief of Bob's pain was noted, so he was prescribed a drug to alleviate psychosis. The consultant at the pain relief unit detected progressive dementia over the years of attendance at the pain clinic and informed his GP each time. Bob was subsequently discharged from the pain relief clinic after five years of attendance. A year later, the GP referred both Bob and his wife to an assessment centre, where he was noted to be slowly dementing and too difficult for his wife to handle. Application was made for exemption from personal community charge on the grounds of severe mental impairment. For the next three years, his worsening aggression presented constantly as crises until he was admitted to the nursing home, four years after the first series of crises.

Three years later, in the nursing home, he was referred to a community psychiatric nurse because of aggression and difficult behaviour, saying he was bored. He was seen again a few months later, found to be less aggressive, more manageable, pleasant and cheerful. He was then discharged from community psychiatry due to their excessive caseload.

Bob was born and grew up in Grimsby, a butcher by trade, and enjoys telling his tale of cycling to Oxford due to lack of work during the depression in the 1930s. His wife and family visited at weekends, including his young granddaughter. He was always 'on his best behaviour' when they visited. Comments in his care plan noted that at times he could be very uncooperative. During these times, the risk of aggression was high, though more likely to be verbal rather than physical. The aim throughout his care, therefore, has been to calm his tendency to verbal aggression. The suggested care plan included reminding him of where he was living and trying to divert him from aggression. This was successful when talking about his youth, and he was found to be best managed with humour, enjoying a joke even when apparently angry. It was deemed necessary to write in his care plan that he be reminded that swearing was not acceptable behaviour, especially in the public spaces of a residential home with many women and visitors present.

Another aspect of his care plan was that of help with all aspects of hygiene. He was especially not keen on bathing, needing encouragement, but was usually continent. Therefore, the care deemed appropriate was assistance with washing and dressing and constant encouragement. Guidance is given for him to be as independent as possible. In his medical notes, which date from his arrival in Oxford, there is a thirty-year history of frequency of micturition (passing small amounts of urine at frequent intervals), which probably accounts for his constantly sore penis. He constantly makes trips to the lavatory and during the study was observed to make over ten visits in an hour. Mention of this is important as one of the areas of life in the nursing home that affects women residents is having to use a unisex toilet after men, some of whom have urinated over the toilet seat and the surrounding floor area. As mentioned in Chapter 2 in the section on poor maintenance and lack of equipment and supplies, this was an issue that upset the women residents. Bob constantly tried to leave the table during meals to go to the WC, something discouraged by the care assistants. Frequently, on his return he had soiled trousers and an open zip, making it obvious where he had been, in the midst of people trying to enjoy a meal. This kind of behaviour demands more attention from care assistants than that given to some of the women with dementia who, as mentioned, are quiet, silent, even muted.

Having noted the case histories of these residents, who are fairly representative of the forty-three in total suffering with dementia, we can see that following on from the institutions of past eras, we have created another type of institution for the older cognitively impaired person, that is, people with severe dementia who cannot manage activities of daily living. This can also be seen in the light of Goffman's 'total institution' (1991) and Foucault's *Madness and Civilisation* (1961). Foucault referred to the incarceration of people post-Enlightenment who had begun to fail to fit into accepted norms of society. The counter-argument is that the care home as an institution is not a prison; the residents are not locked up as a punishment but for their safety. As these people have in fact lost their ability to sense danger, with great risk of wandering off, there is a need for them to be as free from harm as possible, arguably within such an institution as a care home.

The case studies here are not the residents' oral histories, because they were unable to communicate verbally in a way that could be understood clearly. These narratives are gleaned from nursing and medical notes as well as from conversations with relatives, in order to be able to understand what made entry to a nursing home a priority. In particular, these narratives also show how relatives and neighbours reached a crisis point, becoming unable to care for the person in the community, often after many years. The relative detects serious risk to their own state of mind and the quality of life within their family. These evolving crises show an ever-increasing need for an institution, namely a residential home, to provide safety and freedom from danger for people with dementia, a modern-day 'total institution'. If this is so, then the quality of life for the person with dementia, the employee and the other residents needs to be assessed while constantly striving for improvements and equilibrium between individual and institutional needs.

The common features presenting in these crises of nursing home admissions are poor maintenance of personal hygiene, confusion of time and place, inappropriate wandering away from the home environment and a growing disorder of home living conditions. Added to this are aggravating circumstances such as loss of income and poverty, loss of friends and support, depression, an increasing dependency on alcohol and the onset of physical illness. For family, friends and neighbours, there is a reticence to be seen as interfering, even though a desire for solutions is paramount. Relatives and neighbours are often forced into encountering extreme circumstances, such as animal faeces in the home, or the risk of fire from a gas stove being left on. Relatives are often relieved when social services intervene and deliver care provision, but more significantly they are troubled by the 'loss' of the person they knew and loved and the loss of being able to communicate with them.

The quality of life for both the person with dementia and the immediate family and neighbours can deteriorate to the point of exhaustion and even exasperation. In Arthur's case in particular, a worried neighbour had to persist in writing letters to the GP and social services, at times despairing that a solution to what she felt was an intolerable situation would be found and acted upon. The only workable solution for all the residents discussed above appeared to be the provision of institutional care and protection, producing an acceptable quality of life within a twenty-first-century setting.

Dementia within the Nursing Home Setting

All the care plans concerning the residents mentioned in the case histories note that help is needed with activities of daily living such as washing and bathing, and regular escorting to the lavatory. In reality, what does this mean for the nursing home staff? As mentioned in the Introduction, I worked for one year alongside the majority of care assistants, observing their regular routine, especially on the morning shift where staff cared for five residents each. However, due to regular staff sickness and the nearly permanent lack of one nurse on one wing, the number increased to six and on one occasion one care assistant cared for nine residents on the morning shift.

For all the people described in the case histories shown above, the care assistants managed their regular routine with skill and understanding. The residents were well known to them and their needs were often anticipated, even when verbal communication was not possible. However, on the wing without a permanent nurse, the morning routine was noticeable by its disorganisation and somewhat hectic style. Into this setting was admitted a man with a history of dementia. Cecil had no children, his wife died shortly after his admission to the home and his closest family was a nephew. I was able to observe his time of settling in and his regular need for assurance as to time and place. He regularly featured in my field notes about the morning's events, most notably because he constantly asked questions as to what to do next, only to be told to wait for what would happen. By 8.30 a.m., he was still in his dressing gown and pyjamas, and had eaten his breakfast, served to him at 8.15 a.m., and was always restless to be getting dressed but was unable to manage alone. If told to shave with his electric razor, he was unable to manage and habitually became distressed.

One of the policies within the home is that no residents are washed and dressed by night staff (whose shift ends at 8 a.m.), only and always by day staff. The Head of Care, as well as many of the care assistants, said that when this decision was made, it was to give the residents the dignity of not having to get up and be dressed extremely early in the morning. In particular, it was felt that the residents in their own homes would not 'get up at the crack of dawn'. There are many anecdotal accounts within nursing and among staff of care homes that say this kind of practice is seen to be of assistance to the day staff, in the belief that the patient or resident would not necessarily know how early it was in the day. So leaving residents to be attended to by the day staff stemmed from the desire to be rid of what was seen to be a 'bad' practice, making the resident's dignity paramount.

Cecil

Cecil had been in government service all his career and most certainly would have started his day much earlier than he was expected to in the nursing home. His constant worrying about what he should do next between 7.30 a.m. and when he was dressed was always answered with phrases such as 'in a minute', or 'when I've done Bill'. His anxiety then increased and he would ask anyone, staff or resident, what to do next. He may have benefited from an appraisal of his previous lifestyle and routine, which could then have been incorporated into his care plan. If, for instance, a member of the night staff helped him wash and dress at 7.15 a.m. and took fifteen minutes to do so, then this would not have coincided with the two shifts handing over at 8 a.m.

Managers of other institutions say how difficult it is to change entrenched routines and working methods among staff. This is especially so when the care assistants have been in post for many years. As it was, on the day in the week that he was bathed, Cecil was often still in his nightclothes at 10.30 a.m., resulting in a heightened state of anxiety. On one occasion, I heard him say to the housekeeper, 'I think it is unbelievable that I have been kept waiting'. It did occur to me then that as a high-ranking civil servant before he retired, it would have been rare for him to be kept waiting. That, along with the fact that he may have been an early riser and certainly dressed before 8.30 a.m. each day, could well account for his anxiety. Even though his career biography as a policeman was known, an interpretation of his preferred routines had either not been undertaken or not considered when the care plan was made. More importantly, the nurse in charge of the wing, who would have devised routines and care plans and informed the care assistants accordingly, had left and the post was unfilled. The care assistants, without the kind of training and acquired skills necessary, or even the authority, were unable to address those particular needs. The residents with dementia, who were compliant with their given routine, including waiting to be washed and dressed each day, were not seen to present problems.

Although he was perceived to be a problem, Cecil was rarely given any explanation as to his morning routine; with his dementia increasing in severity, communication was problematic anyway. Considering the morning workload, one could see why Cecil was not always given an answer to his constant questions, but with training and a higher ratio of staff to residents it may have been possible for the care assistants to alleviate his anxiety. Cecil was also seen to be demanding, which for the care assistant meant a 'heavier workload'. Whether as part of his personality or due to his dementia, the inability to wait when asked was wearying for care assistants. Once, on leaving the home, I went to say goodnight to the residents, whereupon Cecil wanted me to sit with him and tell him what was expected of him and what he was to do. On explaining that I would be back tomorrow when we could sit together and I would listen to him, he retorted sharply and with anger, saying, 'Oh all of you always get it wrong, because it's not me that has the worries, it's all of you pestering me'. There was frequently a sense of anger, even when he was 'sitting quietly', and care assistants were aware of this, with a white-knuckle tension seen in him at times. The routine of the nursing home must have contrasted greatly with his disciplined career, and there was the added fact that he did not have to interact with as many women previously as he did since living in the home.

There was usually one male nurse, two maintenance men and one male cleaner along with nine women care assistants on day duty. The kitchen staff members were all women, as were most of the domestic staff. The management was all female until later in the study, and only eighteen out of seventy-six residents were men. Cecil was moved to another wing after striking up a relationship with a woman resident (as described in Chapter 2). There were two other male residents on the wing Cecil was moved to who liked to talk with staff and visitors but did not communicate much with each other. When in the lounge, Cecil was seated near them and not surrounded by women as in the other lounge. Also, there were more senior care assistants on this wing, including two women who had worked for nearly twenty years in the home and had acquired many skills in interpreting the needs of residents who could not verbally express what they were feeling or thinking, often only expressing themselves through frustration and anger. For Cecil, his morning routine immediately became more ordered and regular on this wing, and he became less anxious.

It seemed to me that what Cecil most needed in the nursing home was a sense of routine, even if different from that of his life at home. Some residents with dementia had a regular routine provided for them by a skilled care assistant or nurse, while others such as Cecil, new to the home, seemed to flounder in the midst of many routines. John Bayley, Wharton Professor of English at the University of Oxford, wrote movingly in *The Times* newspaper of the routine of Christmas, shared with his wife, the novelist and philosopher Iris Murdoch, who has since died of Alzheimer's disease:

> For years my wife and I have taken the same walk every Christmas – into Kensington Gardens and past the Round Pond. The scenery is at its best on a bright winter's morning. We wander down to the Serpentine … Coming home to a snug lunch – usually sardines and bacon and eggs – a certain amount to drink and a good rest, a feeling of quite uninspiring peacefulness prolongs itself in the mild night air. The increasing warmth of winter in London seems more noticeable now – how many years since it snowed at Christmas. I ask my wife, Iris, if she can remember. She can't. She is tranquilly enjoying the Christmas repose, looking forward to getting back to work on her book on philosophy after Boxing Day. But wait a moment … that was years ago … she doesn't remember any of it now. Yet our Christmas rituals go onwards the same, a peaceful and blessed routine. Routine is a saving necessity for many elderly people who suffer fading memory and the illness which has now been recognised as Alzheimer's, the illness which my wife now has. For her, routine provides a substitute for memory. It soothes the anxieties of a husband who has come to dread more than anything – more even than the tears and the sentences without meaning – the questions, 'Where are we? Who is coming? What are we doing now?' … Familiarity can take over from memory up to a point. We have done all the usual things. We shall continue for a while to do them. (Bayley 1997)

There is evidence here of a dignity within 'routine', although of course the routine of walking around the Serpentine seems a more acceptable one than aspects of the routine found in the nursing home. It became increasingly more obvious that Cecil needed a customary and scheduled routine that was suitable for him or he would never begin to settle into his new way of life in the home.

This routine and repetition were important to people such as Philippa, a woman resident suffering from profound short-term memory loss. She and I were discussing whether her house had been sold and if her furniture had gone. She told of the need to know, even though she would soon forget, and with insight said to me, 'Even if I am forgetful I still need to know and be told what is happening to me'. She had been a school headmistress, remembering those years well, but forgetful of where she most recently lived. When her minister of religion visited her, she had to be reminded always of who he was but stressed that she was glad to be prompted. On every remembrance, this always caused her to cry, sometimes uncontrollably. On occasions when she was forgetful of time and place and day, it was found helpful for someone to sit with her and read from a book of devotions, such as those written by Mother Teresa, that the home purchased for her and others. Staff did not often have time to sit and read to her, so as part of my role as volunteer helper, I willingly undertook these readings as she and others found solace in them.

Reminiscence and Memory: Living with Short-Term Memory Loss

Nora

Occasionally, when sitting with residents in the lounge or on beginning the day with a greeting, a resident such as Nora would offer information about herself, addressing no one in particular. On one occasion, she told me that she was one of ten children, all her sisters older than her and the brothers younger. Her father had worked in a shoe factory in Northamptonshire but did not bring much money home as 'he spent most of it on drink'. Her mother died when she was fifteen years old and she remembers an older sister coming to school to take her home to be with her. She recalled how at the start of the war she worked in an aircraft parts factory, cycling seven miles daily to the aerodrome. Those were the happiest years of her life, she said, as the women were able to dance with men other than their husbands and boyfriends, as 'this was wartime', and how when the men came home they would not allow it. She said that many women during the war years had had their taste of freedom, only to have it taken away when the men returned. These were poignant moments shared, as after the birth of her only child she was admitted to a psychiatric hospital diagnosed with schizophrenia and remained there for years. She fondly recalls the hospital dances and when sitting for long periods of time, as she often does, she thinks of the past and her memories, but she said she prefers to reminisce in company. She was not from the county where the home was situated, only moving to it on the closure of a psychiatric halfway house, to be near her son and daughter-in-law. She was very sad at losing contact with fellow residents at the halfway house, where she lived after the psychiatric hospital, two of whom had also spent years in the hospital with her and who were felt to be closer than family members.

Emilia

The daughter of another resident, Emilia, told me in detail how her mother had worked in an Oxfordshire village in the manor house. As this house is now a well-known restaurant, we were able to talk of this often with Emilia and prompt her memories of the village and what it was like to work in the manor. On these occasions, she was always animated and got to know my voice and presence as one who would sit with her and talk about her past. Once she mentioned how lonely she was feeling, so the care assistants and I sat and encouraged her to talk about her past at the manor and in the village. She responded to prompts about her daughters and grand-daughters and always replied, 'How lovely', when recognising a name or situation we talked about. She had rich memories of polishing silver, the children of the family at the manor and how she met her husband in the village. She, like one other resident, had come to the county from another part of England to take up a job in service during the economic depression of the 1930s. Her family had intended writing some of her memories down and regretted not doing so while her memory was intact. One of the more lucid residents from another wing, who always lunched on this wing, told me that she did not want to sit with Emilia one lunchtime when I was helping direct residents to their seats. Her reason, upon being asked, was that 'she was funny in the head'. The care assistants objected to this, pointing out that although Emilia did not speak much, often only to ask where she was, she was 'no bother to anyone'. In fact, she was ninety-one years of age, still fairly mobile and like the care assistants say, 'no bother to anyone'. Although at times she did not know which season it was, saying how warm it was for February when it was actually June, she never appeared demanding to the staff. In fact, the care assistants always looked upon Emilia in a sympathetic way, understanding how she was unable to communicate verbally what she wanted. When chatting with Emilia one day about the past, another resident sitting nearby observed that 'it's better than talking about the present', to which all within earshot heartily agreed. This woman represents an important aspect of the study. In order to be able to converse with people with dementia living in the nursing home, and thereby include them in the study, it became necessary for me to know something of their biography. This was not only given gratefully by relatives, but access to medical notes was facilitated by senior staff, where more extensive histories than in the care notes were recorded during the course of a person's lifetime.

Reactions to People with Dementia

Mary

Friends of Mary, another resident who had also been 'in service', told me she was very quiet by nature. Though she smiled a lot and was active physically, she was rarely heard to speak. When seated at an un-laid dining table, she would 'shadow dust' constantly. Two dining tables are located in a lounge, so she often sat there instead of in the easy chairs. Once I encountered Rowena, another resident, encouraging all the women seated in a semi-circle with her to 'round on Mary'. Evidently the main ringleader of this, Rowena, encouraged them all to shout at Mary, 'all together after three'. In loud voices in unison, they all shouted 'Stop it Mary!' Mary looked shocked but within minutes continued her imaginary dusting. Upon asking the group of women, especially Rowena, what concerned them so much, all agreed that it 'got on their nerves' and the ringleader stated that there 'should be places for these people to go to'. Some of the women in the group had been diagnosed with early dementia, some classed as 'confused', but all told me that they thought Mary's repetitive behaviour was unacceptably annoying and affected their peace of mind. On other occasions, when doors banged incessantly in the corridor, they would say loudly that this too 'got on their nerves'. Even one of the quieter ones would say, 'Noisy buggers, it's enough to make a vicar swear'. At the time that Mary was shouted at by the other residents, a care assistant and I walked her to another chair at a different table. Both she and Emilia wished only to sit in the high-back chairs at dining tables, not the lounge chairs, which may well indicate their years 'in service' with little time to relax. An article on how the behaviour of people with dementia can be interpreted describes a woman in day care before admission to residential care. She was given 'jobs' to do, with her personal history as cook/house-keeper at a boys' school in mind. Apparently, this form of activity 'held' her attention:

> The most important props for Enid proved to be dusters or cleaning cloths. Strategically placed they drew Enid in to a meaningful activity in the form of actual dusting or merely changing the position of the cloths. Undertaking these activities helped Enid to feel a sense of value and agency. (Dewing and Garner 1998: 15)

Miller more recently shows that residents benefited from this kind of activity, in her aptly entitled paper 'Beyond Bingo' (Miller 2016).

Cheryl

Another incident that highlighted the impatience of some residents towards others took place when Cheryl was being particularly noisy. This is a lady with severe dementia and little ability to communicate other than by shouting or wailing. She can be calmed by someone sitting and talking with her, but due to shortage of staff and the busy routine of the mornings, this was not always possible. On one occasion, Cheryl was sitting in the conservatory within shouting distance of a dining room and lounge. When she had been shouting for a while, the same group of women mentioned above said they were extremely fed up with it and again used the phrase, 'It gets on my nerves'. One of the women again said, 'There should be places for people like that'. During afternoons, when the occupational therapist was working in the common dining area from which the conservatory led off, Cheryl was left in her room seated alone, so her episodic shouting would not disturb other residents. If a radio was playing music in her room, some of the staff said they felt she was not so alone but did express their concern at Cheryl being alone so much and not in company. At times, her husband expressed his concern over this as well, but always pointed out how he understood the need for it as there did not seem to be other solutions offered. The person complaining about Emilia sitting at the same dining table, as described earlier, was eighty-four years of age, lucid and mobile, and seen by the care assistants to 'have one complaint too many'. She would also be disturbed at the shouting, but was able to turn her hearing aid off so as not to hear it. However, it was observed that, at times, it was difficult for some of the more lucid residents to tolerate the kind of incident described here. Guides to standards in residential care (Residential Forum 1996; Mulley et al. 2015) mention this, saying that in a home where people with dementia live alongside other people with different illnesses, there is an unavoidable tension as the lucid resident often finds it difficult to tolerate the behaviour associated with dementia.

As can be seen by some of the situations here described, staff and residents, as well as myself, were able to communicate with some of the residents with dementia and at times actually hold conversations. However, the kind of conversation that some of the residents with dementia were able to have is seen in the following account, which shows how difficult it can be for staff addressing this on a daily basis and the impact it can have on the quality of their working lives.

Another conversation took place among the women previously mentioned sitting in a group. Meg, a resident in the early stages of dementia, joining them one morning at 10.30 a.m., said that she 'had not felt right since having my bath and hair washed'. One of the women exclaimed, 'How awful! Do they have to do that to you?' meaning, 'Do you have to be washed and dressed?' Although harmless and certainly involving communication, this kind of conversation can take its toll on lucid residents, showing that with many of the residents the staff are not able to converse other than at the most superficial level. Care assistants and nurses alike spoke of the weariness that comes from coping with such different levels of communication on a daily basis, often for months and years. It seems to me that this weariness is also associated with the lack of training in skills needed to work with people with dementia. Once, sitting with Cecil near a window overlooking the garden, he wanted answers to where he was and why he was there. He fairly lucidly pointed out how confused and disoriented he often feels. I had prompted this discussion by commenting on his good position overlooking the garden, but he answered that he did not recognise this garden, going on to say how isolated he felt, how age had caught up with him and how his 'best years were over'. He asked me if he was boring me, and asked me for answers to why he felt so isolated, so I asked him if any friends would visit him. He said that he had no friends, which may possibly tie in with being retired or even his pre-morbid personality. I admit to feelings of inadequacy at times with Cecil and his constant questioning and need for reassurance, and can see how some of the less experienced staff were quick to 'fob off' his questions. Because of the constancy of the questioning whenever he saw someone enter the lounge, if I was feeling weary I would sometimes avoid saying goodnight to residents in that lounge before leaving. There was empathy, therefore, when care assistants were unable to attend to Cecil's demands. Although it was difficult to accept that his requests or demands may be ignored, I could empathise with the negative feelings that began to emerge, as there seemed no solution to how to attend to him in the midst of many other demands upon staff time.

Generally, afternoons in the nursing home followed a less hectic pace than the mornings, and it was during moments such as these that care assistants would take time to explain to residents with dementia where they were living and why. For example, while one of the care assistants was preparing the tea cups on the trolley to give out afternoon tea, she quietly explained to Glenys, who was hovering nearby, where the home was, where the river was, where she was living and why. This resident had been told on admission to the home, by both family and social worker, that she was only being admitted for a holiday. When the perceived time for a holiday had passed, Glenys restlessly and constantly asked to go home, so her key worker in the home would often encourage her and remind her of where she was, truthfully answering questions about when she was going home, if ever.

Many of the care assistants who had worked for a long time with people with dementia in the home were able to address the kinds of needs seen in

Cecil, but some of the staff, younger and new to the work of caring, and often without training, were unable to do so. Residents with needs such as those shown by Philippa, who sobbed at being informed that her house was sold, were attended to with ease because they were seen to be much less demanding than people such as Cecil. Also, it was 'easier' to comfort someone's sorrow and bouts of crying rather than defuse the bouts of anger and aggression shown by some residents. One morning, Rose, a resident who had lived in the home for a few months, was looking sad and anxious. One of the kitchen staff tried to buoy her along with jokes and light-hearted words. Rose was asked if she had her 'happy head on or her awkward head' that day, which sounded tactless to all in earshot. I sat and talked with this resident, only to find out that her house and furnishings were being sold that same day. Even without training in listening to people with dementia, many of the staff acquired the skills necessary, but the busy workload, including that of the kitchen staff, does not often allow for knowledge, such as what was happening to this particular resident, to filter through as it happens.

Two separate families voiced delight at their relatives being able to 'wander' freely and rarely encountering danger within the nursing home. One resident, Evelyn, had been living in a different residential home in the same county, but the residents there needed temporary accommodation while the refurbishment of that home took place. Evelyn's daughters mentioned that they found her to be freer to walk around the temporary home than where she had been living, and because of this sense of freedom wanted her to move to the temporary home permanently. This she was able to do, to the satisfaction of both family and staff. Evelyn had been an active woman, running her own hotel and playing tennis. On most days at 2.30 p.m., she could be seen walking to the tea trolley laid out for 3 p.m. tea, helping herself to a cake and sitting contentedly in the conservatory eating it. Her independent spirit was not curtailed in that all staff felt willing to let her do this. The staff and I discussed the kind of freedom to walk around the hotel in her days as the owner, acknowledging that to curtail this choosing of her cake earlier than tea time would have been detrimental to her independence. However, no other residents did likewise; when other free spirits offered to wash the dishes, for example, they were discouraged from doing so and therefore curtailed somewhat in their independence.

Dementia as Challenging Behaviour

'Wandering' is sometimes seen to present as a problem in the nursing home setting and is seen to be an invasion of personal as well as public space. The term is usually used to describe a series of behaviours manifest in people diagnosed with dementia or other cognitive disorders. 'Wandering' is also a person's inability to return to her or his point of origin, frequently a searching process, which happens within the setting of the nursing home and the danger of a busy main road with a fifty miles per hour speed limit at the end of the drive. This is especially hazardous if the resident follows their carer outside, unbeknown to the staff member. This 'wandering' takes its emotional toll on a busy workforce, often made busier by a shortage of staff.

'Wandering' can be seen to be aimless, restless and searching. Care assistants in particular were able to interpret the reasons for 'wandering' and try to answer them accordingly, instead of resorting to medication. What seems to be most important is whether this kind of behaviour is, in fact, a way of self-expression or non-verbal communication. As shown in Chapter 2, for example, it only takes an intuitive named care assistant to interpret that Arthur's pacing behaviour expresses his need to defecate. In interpreting his needs, she conferred dignity upon him and showed a coping strategy in dealing with the challenging behaviour of much shouting and wandering, where coping strategies are not always easy to implement.

Of all the challenging behaviour observed in the nursing home, aggression is the most difficult to tolerate as well as to deal with. It is worth considering the reasons for aggression. The challenging behaviours noted have been chosen to highlight the recurrent reasons for onset of aggression observed in the nursing home. It occurred most consistently during times of intimate care, such as bathing, dressing or shaving, and importantly resulted from the person not understanding what was happening to him or her and especially if not wanting to be dressed. An illustration of verbal aggression would be the kind of swearing Arthur and Bob aimed at the care assistants who regularly attended them, when they did not want a morning shave. However, it should also be possible for allowances to be made for someone 'getting out of bed the wrong way'. Likewise, as mentioned above, flexibility should be possible, for example allowing Cecil to get dressed earlier than normal, which could see his frustration and anger ebb. I have heard it said that we should recognise a person's right to anger, including someone with dementia. While that is the ideal, it does not always work in open public areas such as dining rooms or sitting rooms, in that it is frightening for other residents, untrained staff members, relatives and visitors. During all outbursts of anger and aggression observed, it was the calm diffusion of it, without resorting to physical or drug-induced restraints, that impressed both visitors and the researcher alike. Not once was restraint observed or recounted, which can only testify to the way the outbursts were managed.

The kind of continued shouting outbursts from Cheryl and the type of questioning demands shown by Cecil did impact on other residents' lives, but they were usually tolerated. There was some evidence of residents distancing themselves, as with the resident who did not want Emilia to dine with her because 'she was funny in the head', as described earlier. Another example of distancing can be found in Cheryl being kept for long periods of time in her room so that there would be some alleviation of the noise caused by her shouting and distress. Some distancing was present, but more often than not there was a sympathetic tolerance and a sense of sadness that a lucid resident could not hold conversations with the person with dementia. The sadness was more apparent if the residents had known each other prior to admission.

Considering that aggression, shouting and other challenging behaviour take place in the public spaces of the lounge or dining areas, it was not difficult to observe how this impacted on residents and staff alike. Differences in behaviour between the women and men suffering from dementia were also evident, with the women usually communicating in quieter ways than the men.

Chapter 2
CARING IN ACTION
WOMEN IN THE WORKPLACE

> It is the meaning that men attribute to their life, it is their entire system of values that define the meaning and the value of old age. The reverse applies: by the way in which a society behaves towards its old people it uncovers the naked and often carefully hidden truth about its real principles and aims.
> —Simone de Beauvoir, *Old Age*

Care assistants, more than nurses, form the major part of the workforce within the home, as shown in other studies in residential nursing/care homes. A common feature within the workforce of these residential homes is the predominance of women. At the time of the study, all the care assistants, thirty-two in number, were women, and of six nurses, one was male. Bank (temporary) staff nurses were all women, as were the four kitchen staff. Three women and one man were cleaners, two women worked in the laundry, the housekeeper was a woman, and home maintenance was carried out by two men. The manager, the head of care and deputy head of care were all female, as was the administrative clerk. All but one of the residents were on the list of one GP practice which had three male doctors and one female. This gender distribution within the workforce is echoed in care homes throughout the county, where the male perspective is not often present.

Ethnicity among staff in this Oxfordshire nursing home does not follow the trend of the UK residential care sector in employing care assistants from a variety of cultures and ethnicities. All the care assistants in the present home were white, female working class, except one woman from the South Pacific. The only male nurse originated from West Africa, the nursing home being his first and only employment in this country. His wife, also from West Africa, worked as a night nurse in the home within a predominantly British white nursing and care staff.

All residents in the study were white British women and men from a variety of backgrounds, predominantly working class. One Caucasian man born and brought up in Germany had spent all his married life in the UK. No resident was from an ethnic minority group. Near the end of the study, the minor shareholder, a medical doctor and Hindu in origin, bought out the major shareholder, both being South Asian male entrepreneurs. Two English businessmen were appointed as financial and administrative consultants. The home then became the only care home within that group of hotels run by an Indian businessman. Some years later, after the time of fieldwork, the male nurse was appointed head of care, one young man became permanently employed as a care assistant and another young man worked temporarily as a care assistant, during his summer vacation from university.

Within the context of this chapter, it is not only the resident, mainly older women who feature, but also the paid carers, who as women interact with them daily. Paid care work is best understood as work first and caring second, in that care/work employment as a care assistant is constructed within established ideas of family roles, informal care as well as characteristics attributed to gender roles.

As with nursing, the job of a paid carer, namely a care assistant, is ambiguous. In this nursing home, care assistants outnumbered nurses four to one and so undertook many tasks similar to those undertaken by nurses. However, without professional training, the care assistant has a different perspective, coming from a model that most of the care assistants in the study knew best, that of motherhood. These women said that without training, they saw their job as an extension of their family role, which most significantly for the resident is primarily one of child care and parenting. This is not without its problems when considering the infantilisation of older people, when their choices and decisions are made for them. Here, motherhood as the model for caring is questioned as to its suitability in that mothering is based on the relationship model of kin, whereas caring is 'mothering' by a stranger. I am not questioning the model of motherhood as a suitable framework for care, but rather the assumption that motherhood provides carers with the necessary and appropriate skills for care work. This need to be cared for in all activities of daily living (ADLs) in old age, therefore, becomes more tolerable when met by a stranger than when undertaken by a relative. The ability deemed to be necessary to work as a carer is itself filled with gender role stereotyping, in that mothering and caring have much in common. Hockey and James (1993), when discussing infantilisation as social discourse, showed that use of the parenting comparison is a coping strategy involved with the one-sided power relationship that the carer holds. Focusing on a dependency model within the care of older adults, they show how an individual's power and autonomy can be lost.

Caring is difficult to define but is socially understood as being associated with the physical care for a person, including much bodily contact. This paid care work is about creating 'order out of disorder' and this chapter looks at how this was achieved and performed in the care home, and in particular how the care assistants and nurses interacted with the residents.

Caring and the Care Assistant

For the seventy-six residents in the nursing home, there was a desired total of eleven care assistants and two qualified nurses for the heaviest shift, namely the morning one. Forty care assistants in total are employed, with twelve of that number allocated to night duty shifts alone. Five care assistants out of the twelve worked on any given night shift, plus two nursing staff. One can therefore see from these figures that the bulk of the 'caring' work is undertaken by the care assistants and not the nurses.

As an outsider, I attempt to understand the dynamics, tensions and strains involved in caregiving, showing that the central role is performed by care assistants as the main caregivers and that the interactions between the care assistants and the residents result in narratives of a shared world. What is highlighted in this chapter is the total interdependence between employees and residents and its particular sensitivities. Throughout all the observations, it was apparent that the quality of life for the resident was dependent on the quality of the working life for the employee, thus illustrating how the two are inextricably linked. By working with individual care assistants and subsequently writing on the many aspects of their care, the importance is shown here of the need for sensitivity to the difficulties faced by both care assistants and residents within a residential setting.

One of the most significant issues to consider when looking at care assistants and their caregiving is that of training and acquiring the skills necessary to do the job. For many of these care assistants, no formal training had been offered during their employment and only became an issue within recent decades. It is evident from the care assistants interviewed and observed that an ethic of care exists within nearly all of them. There is also evidence of skills being acquired 'on the job', which in many were excellent, but in others lacking. Working on the premise that most women can and do care for family members, the care given could be seen to be an extension of the role these women play in their home lives.

When working with the care assistants, it is noticeable that what they do for the residents is extremely similar to the role of the nurses. They face the physical dependency of residents upon them just as nurses do and, especially with residents with dementia, who are often bemused as to what is happening, they face multiple situations such as dealing with someone who appears unaware why they are in the home, as well as being hit, verbally abused and having to be ready to find a resident who may have wandered outside alone. This emphasises the strain and stresses that care assistants encounter in their everyday work. By working alongside the care assistants, it was possible to observe the difficulties they faced, including tension and pressures, heightened by the lack of training. Add to this the care assistants' feeling that a lot of what their job consists of has traditionally been a 'nurse's job', and a cauldron of angst is seen to come to the surface, especially in times of regular staff shortages. Coping mechanisms within many aspects of the work are highlighted.

Both the head of care (a nursing post) and the care assistants themselves agreed for me to work alongside them in their daily roles, especially on the morning shift, always the busiest time of day, when residents were assisted in getting out of bed and helped with washing and dressing. No care assistant objected to our working together or to the examples of care being written into the study. All the care assistants knew that I had trained as a nurse and, as we worked alongside each other, parts of my biography as a nurse and researcher as well as a person and colleague were shared with them. In return, they too shared much of their personal history.

Patterns of Care

The following examples will show what is involved in caring for residents, and from these case studies it will be seen that the ethos of care runs through the work of even the most informally trained care assistant. Two of the female care assistants had been working within this same institution for over two decades. Two others had worked there for ten years. Although there were no formal senior care assistant positions, these two older women and others on different shifts are seen to be 'senior' in terms of their acquired wealth of knowledge over years in the job. Much 'training', therefore, is conducted during routine care of residents, as new care assistants are assigned to work alongside them in order to gain the skills necessary to carry out the tasks.

I wished to fit in as unobtrusively as possible, and the first day working with a care assistant is a fair example of how this was achieved. On arrival, the staff members were serving breakfast, so rather than get in the way of an established routine, I made toast for the residents and then collected up the crockery while the care assistant went for a quick break. This first informal break, if only for a cigarette, is seen as important in that there is no formal handover time from night to day care staff and this is where a crucial exchange of information takes place before the busy morning work gets underway. Although one care assistant was back at work after time off sick, the staff were still one care assistant short as another was ill at home.

Two care assistants said they used to take on the extra work of bathing, as well as the daily washing and dressing of residents when someone was off sick, until she and a colleague decided that 'enough was enough'. From then on, they attended to other residents when short of staff, but would only bath their 'own quota', as they otherwise felt the workload to be unacceptable and feared that the regular care of their 'own' residents would decline. The reason for their decision was that they felt management 'took them for granted', that the situation 'had gone on for too long' and, more importantly, that their 'own' residents were suffering as the level of caregiving was not as it would be with their normal workload. By caring for more residents than usual, less time was taken with each individual.

Maddie, a senior care assistant, showed much common sense in her work method and I was able to see what is entailed in getting at least six people up and dressed each day. When bathing Ina, she shampooed her hair thoroughly, gently and with evident care. Her organisational skills and practical common sense were probably as much to do with her personality as with her many years of experience. For example, after washing the long hair of one resident in the bath and rinsing it with the shower hose, she then tied it up on top of the woman's head so that it would not trail in the dirty water of her bath. In the mornings when she got those residents up from bed who were not due to be bathed, she gave a full body wash, always rinsing well. She chose their clothes efficiently if they could not choose for themselves, and quickly consulted the resident as to their preference where possible. All the time she talked, explaining what she was doing, constantly conducting her work in a caring way. After each person was ready and seated in a lounge, she made them a cup of tea, as the next round of hot drinks would not be served until 11 a.m., when all the 'chores' were done. This was an individual touch, as not all care assistants were inclined or felt able to do so, though two other carers poured a cold drink for their residents after finishing the personal tasks and taking them to their seat in the lounge. An individual feature shown by Maddie when bathing residents was to leave them to sit and soak in the bath for a few minutes and not hurry them. The attention she showed to detail and practical understanding in getting the residents up is seen, for example, with their hold-up stockings – she twists them at the top and tucks them in to stay up when they have lost their elasticity. She, like most of the care assistants, made each bed as she went along, taking the linen off the bed of those who had a bath, ready to make up with clean linen later in the shift, probably in the early afternoon. During such tasks, we got to know each other, sharing personal histories. This particular care assistant is a family woman with well-loved grandchildren of her own. As we shared with each other our life experiences, especially concerning families, it was evident that within her family she is seen as a practical, caring person ready to help her own children and grandchildren, and generally available to them as they live nearby. There is a sense that she uses this practical approach in her work situation, as well as the acquired knowledge gained from many years of work. When she had joyous news to share of an addition to the family, or sad news such as the illness of her father, it was shared not only with colleagues but with residents as well, thus including them vicariously in her family life.

During the hours of working with residents and their principal carers, we shared much about our lives, including the residents in our discussions. Some of the residents, able and interested enough to have conversations with the care assistants about their family life, became involved in these encounters. They had a wealth of experience to share from their own lives while the work was carried out. Some of the employees have very serious issues to contend with at home. For example, Valerie spoke about trouble at the primary school her seven-year-old son attended, where the headmistress was seen to 'pick on him' regularly. Even the other schoolchildren noticed but were 'too scared to tell', until it was reported and investigated. The outcome was that both child and parents attended a child psychiatric unit as outpatients, where the teacher was also interviewed, and the care assistant told us that the health professionals then informed the family that they 'found her to be a very difficult woman'. The care assistant had felt 'angry and frightened' by the whole incident, and in recounting it well after the event told of how she was carrying a 'burden' at the time. Other writers note the kinds of worries that employees bring to their working situation each day, well known in Hochschild's (1989) words as 'the second shift' – an apt description for care assistants. This 'second shift' relates to employees managing their own households as well as child care arrangements, which at times can be tenuous. Of the care assistants who had children of school age, mainly boys, most mentioned their worries about them 'getting into bad company' after school hours, when they as mothers were unable to be at home and worryingly did not always know where their boys were.

One notable aspect of working with the care assistants was that although I slowed them down in their work due to discussion and explanations about their work, their assurances that they did not mind were genuine. All showed much interest in what the study was about and how it would highlight aspects of their lives, including aspects of quality of life for them as employees. In return, I helped with all aspects of the work, and although I did not lift heavy residents, I performed all other tasks, such as helping to wash and dress residents, the emptying of commodes and making beds. When working with Valerie, who had many years of experience and is of a quiet personality, the caring is evident. One resident she looks after has psoriasis (a skin complaint), so cream must be applied by the care assistant. This was done in a systematic and methodical fashion, ensuring that all areas affected were covered. This resident has lived in the home for a year, but Valerie, her named care assistant, only recently received information about the need to ensure that she does routine leg exercises. Valerie said that this poor communication is prone to happen because there is no specific handover between care staff, only between the nurses, hence the need for the informal early morning break which took place in the staff smoking room.

There was a constant movement of care assistants to help each other lift residents when bathing and washing them. There was an unwritten agreement among themselves that, when needed, they help each other with certain aspects of the job, especially lifting. Residents as well as employees were seen to benefit from this sharing of the workload. In a way, this learning on the job is all part of the 'socialisation' into the unwritten rules of the workforce. Being unwilling to help was viewed negatively by other care assistants. Even when I worked alongside care assistants, they continued to seek help with lifting from their colleagues, as they all thought it was a task that I should not be involved with. Inexperienced lifting with unfamiliar equipment can result in both staff and residents being injured.

On another day working with Valerie, she explained that sometimes one of the nurses would ask the care assistant to attend to two of her residents as well as her own, resulting in a heavier than normal workload. One of those residents routinely had her hair washed on a different day from her bath, as she enjoyed 'going to the hairdressers', even though it took place within the home. This gives some indication of flexibility in the routine of the home, even during the busy morning routine. When one of the residents in the care assistant's allocation died, she envisaged a slightly lighter workload, but by having to do the nurse's two residents, she was not able to stop for a coffee break until 11.45 a.m. As with many institutions and ward situations, a coffee break is not taken by the staff until all residents and patients are up and dressed. Two 'senior' care assistants take time to stop for a quick cup of coffee on the way round, during which time they go outside for a cigarette, which they and others feel is acceptable. The manager also accepts this as unofficial practice, while emphasising that the work routine should not suffer because of it.

On being asked why all residents had to be attended to before lunch, even when the care assistants were busy during times of staff shortage, the care assistants said there was little flexibility and that 'the manager wanted it that way'. The two senior care assistants pointed out, however, that their practice of bathing someone in the afternoon if he or she proved to be 'difficult' or did not want a bath enabled their own flexibility of routine within the organisation. The 'quick' cup of coffee and cigarette taken between attending to residents is also evidence of this type of flexibility. The 'flexibility' described here is similar to that Lee-Treweek calls 'resistance', which, in her view, is seen in the nursing auxiliaries' ambiguous relationship to authority as 'an acceptance of one's place in and yet at other times a resistance to the hierarchy' (Lee-Treweek 1997: 54). She showed how the staff used resistance as a daily coping strategy, enabling them to get through and apply some control over their work. The care assistants told me that they are not bound to an authoritarian routine, rather they present themselves as the instigators of a meaningful routine and the maintenance of it. The care assistants would work around this routine, for example bathing Arthur in the afternoons when it is quieter compared to the busy mornings. More time could be given to him then, especially in encouraging him not to be aggressive towards them. In this way, they made the work easier for themselves as well as for a resident like Arthur who needed much time and attention.

There are, however, ambiguities even in the use of the term 'caring'. The position can hold power over the weak and vulnerable and yet can be disempowering for the employee such as the care assistant, or even the relative caring for a family member at home. For the care assistant, the low pay and hard work are consistently described as stressful. The perceptions of the job associated with low social status can produce a sense of powerlessness. When on duty, not having time to meet their own needs during staff shortages, such as having a cup of coffee, can add to feelings of frustration in the job and subsequent low morale. Conversely, the care assistant by the very nature of the work of caring for the vulnerable can be seen to be in a position of power within the institution's hierarchy of power. Some of the ideas here can be seen in terms of the French philosopher Foucault's concept of power and power relations. Within the hierarchy of the institution, care assistants are located in the lower echelons. They themselves are at pains to point out that they are the workers at the 'grass-roots' level, one even saying that they are 'at the coal-face' in keeping the system of caregiving going. In terms of power, they were able to exert it within their daily routine by their use of flexibility or 'resistance'. Within Foucault's appraisal of power in western industrialised societies, he addresses questions that people feel deeply about, which can be used to understand those questions faced by the resident within an institution who is seen to have less control over their own life than the employee, especially the care assistant:

Who exercises power? How? On whom? Who makes decisions for me? Who is preventing me from doing this and telling me to do that? Who is forcing me to live in a particular place when I work in another? Who is programming my movements and activities? How are these decisions on which my life is completely articulated taken? All these questions seem to me to be fundamental ones today. And I don't believe that this question of 'who exercises this power' can be resolved unless that other question 'how does it happen?' is resolved at the same time. (Foucault 1988: 102)

Foucault also suggests that power cannot be studied unless 'strategies of power' are looked at, 'the networks, the mechanisms, all those techniques by which a decision is accepted and by which that decision could not but be taken in the way that it was' (Foucault 1988: 104). Here, this can be considered in terms of the bureaucracy evident in the management of institutional life and the way in which employees describe management as authoritative. Bureaucracy can hinder initiative, with the resultant lack of spontaneity usually resulting in a negative outcome for residents and employees. Nevertheless, even where this bureaucracy dampens initiative, some care assistants were observed to be extremely determined, albeit quietly, in their approach to undermine it, such as bathing a resident in the afternoon. No institution such as this could manage without an organisation and routine, especially in ensuring minimal standards of care, but it was what was seen to be bureaucracy for its own sake that had such a discouraging effect on staff morale. What was observed was an over-emphasis on organisation and a task-centred approach which, with the addition of bureaucracy, stifled the creativity of the employee. If bureaucracy is taken to mean the ways in which the home is administered, then much of the dissatisfaction shown by the care assistants and nurses is aimed at the person engaged in administration, namely the manager. Many of the care assistants explained how they did not see the manager as the 'right type' of person for the role. They found her style confrontational, full of criticism and in particular said that she did not 'listen to their point of view'. Linked in with this was their astute perception that she rarely gave out praise, only criticism, something I also witnessed at times. This, of course, is noted in other organisations, not just the care sector, and in all situations is seen to have a wearying effect on the workforce concerned.

Within the attributes associated with the bureaucracy of such an institution, capitalism also has an influence, especially on the quality of life. Studies such as that by Phillipson (1982) show that profit, order and routine are prioritised over and above the individual needs of the resident and certainly above the needs of the staff. This was seen most distinctly while working with a care assistant, Joanna, who discussed some of her concerns with me, particularly one resident's feet. This resident, in an advanced state of dementia, had little capacity to share how she felt, even when in pain. Her toenails were in a desperate state, showing urgent need of chiropody, but she apparently had little money to pay for this. She was privately funded from her own income (controlled by a nephew), having been a woman of independent means from years spent breeding show dogs, but could only have her hair cut occasionally because of this lack of money. A framed photograph in her room of her and the dogs, showing a well-groomed and smartly dressed woman, was but a sad reflection of her present condition. Joanna sensitively expressed how it affects her when she knows that in such a situation as this, all care is not being provided, due to poor organisation rather than a lack of care. For instance, the resident would be eligible for chiropody if she was without personal income and nursing fees, and therefore funded by social services.

A number of care assistants brought in new toiletries and 'extras' for the residents. For instance, one brought her own mother's unwanted vests for one woman. She carries nail clippers, which she thinks the trained staff should do, and commented that in her view some of the nurses do not do as much for their residents as the care assistants do. She cut Millie's nails under protest, as they were definitely in need of a trim. However, Millie, in suffering with dementia, may well have been perplexed, even frightened as to what was happening to her, and was ready to show a certain amount of aggression. She attempted to bite the care assistant for clipping her fingernails, but fortunately was prevented from doing so. In the past, when Nessie, another woman suffering with dementia, was included in the care quota of a trained nurse, two of the care assistants used to bath her as she constantly refused. These refusals had resulted in crusts of dirt and dead skin under her breasts, and she smelt of this decay. It was then decided to allocate her care to a care assistant, thus reiterating the care assistants' belief that they care for the residents in a more holistic way than the trained nursing staff do. This illustrates how care assistants see themselves as the key movers, especially compared to the nurses.

Most of the care assistants thought to ask each resident if I could be present while they attended to them, including while in the bathroom. However, with a few residents it was felt that my presence would make them anxious. On one occasion, it was decided that the care assistant would bath one of the men residents without being observed, as it was felt to be too personal for him to have a relative stranger present. He admitted to not always knowing who various people were, so the care assistant felt that the presence of another person would confuse him. This care assistant, Valerie, worked in a quiet manner with all the residents she looked after, encouraging them to smile, ensuring their contentment even if they were unable to communicate verbally with her. One of the women residents needed regular face cream applied, which the care assistant brought in for her. As she could not find any cream, she used some belonging to another resident who had a number of new creams and cosmetics, brought in by a relative who had recently visited. In this way, the care assistant circumvents the bureaucracy or style of management that does not supply face cream for residents who cannot afford it. However, the person to whom the cream belonged was unable to make decisions and probably would not have been able to answer coherently upon being asked to share her cream, evidence of a lack of autonomy. Echoes of the muted voice are heard here. Lack of opportunity in making decisions occurs with the cognitive decline associated with dementia, resulting in the resident becoming increasingly less consulted about issues to do with her/himself. The issue of face cream shows how care assistants 'beat' the system of having few supplies for the residents and raises another important issue particularly in the care of people who cannot manage to look after themselves. During the study, I did not observe make-up being applied on a woman, and yet men who could not shave themselves had it done for them. Archibald (1994), in an illustrated guide enabling staff to consider people with dementia and their sexuality, discusses the use of clothing and make-up. Although specifically written for staff working with people with dementia, this well applies to all people in residential care, stating that 'the expression of sexuality is about feeling good about ourselves', so how can this best be facilitated? Along with sketches illustrating this good feeling, Archibald writes about clothing:

> How we look and dress is very important to us. In institutions people often seem identical ... How often do we see a row of old ladies with identical hairdos ... What about make-up if a woman has always worn it? ... bright scarves, ties? ... What about encouraging a pride in appearance? (Archibald 1994: 24)

Manoeuvring Difficult Situations

One of the most difficult situations for care assistants to encounter is that classed as 'challenging behaviour'. Dementia, for many sufferers, impacts on their behaviour and manners; they often become aggressive and frightening as a result of confusion. Case studies of this type of behaviour were given prominence earlier, showing the difficult circumstances faced by staff each day that involved 'challenging behaviour' and especially aggression.

Working with an experienced care assistant one lunch time, we noted that one of the female residents became extremely disturbed. She shouted, banging the table forcibly, insisting that she had never ordered eggs and mashed potato, though earlier she had told the kitchen helper that she was 'sick of fish'. There was definite skill shown by the care assistants in diffusing the situation, and any prolonged aggression was avoided by calm, hushed-voice negotiation as to what she felt she should eat. This type of situation happens often, but the care assistants find ways of managing, not necessarily by having formal training, but by inherent skills of personality as well as humour and experience. For instance, one resident was described as being an 'amazing actress today', in trying to avoid a bath, so she did not have one. However, if the care assistant thought that she 'needed one', due to body odour or because she had refused one or more recently, then a whole process of negotiation and encouragement would take place for the bath to be taken/given. Aggression can manifest itself in people with dementia, and of note here is the way in which care assistants influence the patient's behaviour by acknowledging the deterioration inherent in the illness and the adaptation needed to hang on to their remaining capacities. Care assistants like Valerie and Maddie who knew the residents well were seen to regularly negotiate with them so that their aggression and confusion, often the result of their deteriorating condition, could be calmed and soothed, especially in the public areas with visitors present.

Valerie also related an incident that took place during her recent weekend on duty. She described finding a trail of faeces from the lounge to the toilet and another trail leading back to the lounge, rightly guessing that it was Arthur, who was frequently unable to understand where to defecate even when he had found the toilet. Being a Sunday afternoon, the lounge was full of residents and their visitors, many of whom were concerned that the care assistants had to clean it up, acknowledging how busy they had been that day due to a shortage of staff. This relates to discussion of the 'disgust function', as described by Elias (1939) and his important treatise entitled *The Civilising Process*, tracing changing manners since the Enlightenment. He noted how post-medieval European standards concerning speech, table manners, sexual behaviour, bodily functions and violence were increasingly transformed by the rising intolerance of shame and disgust. This 'disgust function' is still evident in society today.

Within the overall question of the quality of life for all residents and the quality of the working life of employees caring for people with dementia, the question of manners and behaviour (especially inappropriate defecation) was of utmost significance. This included Arthur constantly wandering away from where he is safely observed by staff, frequently threatening violence, opening his bowels in inappropriate places as well as his determination to resist a bath. Should the relatively quiet, cooperative, lucid residents, as well as people with dementia of various stages of severity, be subject to the kind of behaviour Arthur shows? It is always more evident during busy times and staff shortage, but if, as management kept stressing, this was the residents' 'home from home', surely such behaviour is inconsistent with this ethos. It was evident that for residents whose frailty intensified and those whose dementia became more severe, tolerance by the other residents rather than irritation and anger was shown more often than not. Staff members daily face extreme mental, emotional and behavioural demands, and although these behaviours can be seen as deviance, it is the often under-qualified care assistants who are the diffusers of such volatile situations. Common sense always seemed to be evident on the part of the care assistant in these situations.

There are units attached to residential homes that are specifically for cognitively impaired people with dementia. These units, while not segregating residents totally, meet most of their daily needs within the unit itself while, on occasions, the staff members bring residents together for concerts and social activities. The care home studied, while not having a separate unit, had many residents classed medically as showing cognitive decline, but who were well integrated into the life of the home.

Without the necessary acquired skills or training in such illnesses and conditions manifesting in such challenging conduct, undue stress and tension for the employees results as they endeavour to negotiate and manage such behaviour. The management of pollution such as defecation, excreta and the control of it is a major if ambiguous part of the care assistant's role. It was this function as manager/mediator that was observed daily when working with care assistants. Most of this mediation and negotiation takes place in the privacy of bedrooms, as noted by Lee-Treweek (1997), who says that it was in the 'private' spaces of the residents' bedrooms that 'the containment of disruption, and the ordering of distress or aggression was carried out', maintaining that the end product of the work was seen to be a 'clean, orderly, quiet resident'. Her description of residential life compares a little harshly when considering the care assistants described here, though the phrase can be applied cautiously in that the 'clean, orderly, quiet resident' leads to considerably less stress for the care assistant when caring for men such as Arthur or Cecil. It is the management of the 'dirt' that Mary Douglas (1966) describes as 'matter out of place' in her analysis of the concept of pollution and taboo in Moses' writings in Leviticus. Always evident in that busy morning routine, the conversion of disorder and chaos into a calm, ordered public space occurred before entry into the public areas of a lounge or hairdressing salon. Though not verbalised in terms such as Mary Douglas's 'matter out of place', an unwritten emphasis on people, clothes and possessions being in their rightful place before coffee time and definitely by lunch time was routinely observed.

The next examples concern containment of difficult situations that represented for the staff daily disorder within the desired calm order of the nursing home. What was significant was the way in which the second example in particular caused so much heated discussion in the home among staff, some residents and their relatives and, at times, the manager.

The situation described in the first example was always carefully managed, especially if the frayed tempers of residents were involved. Frequently, there were insufficient carers on duty to allow them to make the necessary observations concerning one male resident. This account describing a difficult-to-manage situation in the home concerns sexual exploits by one man, and a number of women who were unable to deter his advances. All staff felt that urgent solutions were needed as he was consistently found in women's rooms in incriminating situations, such as with his hand up their skirt or sometimes inside their blouse. He had moderate dementia and since being in the nursing home had consistently behaved in this manner towards female residents, sometimes in public. Staff who knew the situation would go looking for him if they did not know where he was. In this way, the situation was managed. However, they were always cross with him when they found him with women, and especially cross with him when he exposed himself in public, encouraging women residents to fondle him. Twelve of the fourteen women living on that wing were suffering with dementia and not all were able to fend off his behaviour towards them. Some of the other men got cross with him, resulting in an occasional change in his behaviour. These incidents happened on a daily basis and, at times, staff despaired as to what the available solutions were. Other than constantly being aware of where he was, staff said that 'in some respects this residential home caring for both sexes is probably the wrong place for him', recognising that he would be 'managed' better in a unit exclusively for men.

The second example is also to do with sexuality, and considers staff attitudes towards it. Cecil enjoyed the company of women and in particular one woman, Rowena. She had been living in the home for a few years as she was unable to cope alone at home, suffering from short-term memory loss associated with mild dementia. One of the effects of Cecil's profound dementia was that he did not remember that his wife was in fact alive and ill at home. Cecil and Rowena were living on the same wing and became close to each other, although she always called him by a name other than his own, resulting in him being distressed and somewhat confused. They began to hold hands in public, which was considered by all staff to be wrong and one care assistant regularly unclasped their hands if they were sitting together. When intense fondling began to take place, the staff then decided that they should ensure that Cecil and Rowena be seated apart. So, although remaining on the same wing, one was seated in the conservatory and the other in the lounge, which became difficult for the staff to supervise, as Cecil was mobile and although Rowena less so, they were able to seek out each other. During this time, Cecil's wife died though he seemed to show little comprehension of what that meant. Meanwhile, some of the residents started to encourage Cecil and Rowena to 'get married'. This became a game to be played out every day, with Rowena asking when the vicar would arrive to conduct the wedding, and Cecil getting quite angry as he said that Rowena was his wife anyway.

All staff, residents and visitors talked about the situation and news of it spread around the home and community. Staff members said they should be kept apart, but no one offered any other thoughts as to a solution. Some of the regular visitors knew about this, one in particular feeling that too much teasing was being directed at the couple. One evening, residents saw both Cecil and Rowena in their nightclothes lying together in the lounge. Visitors were also present, and the following day a female resident decided to tell the manager. The manager's response was that she was glad to be told of what was happening but would not become proactive in advising staff what to do. One afternoon I asked the manager if this question of sexuality and desire could be seen in ways other than that of controlling the couple concerned and the lack of autonomy involved. She gave examples based on her work in the USA, where residential care she managed had facilities available for two residents to share a private sitting room together. Upon asking her if that could be undertaken in this home, and particularly for Cecil and Rowena so they would be able to cuddle lovingly in private, she painstakingly replied that English mores were different from those of the USA, somewhat 'deli-cate' even, and that this had not 'even begun to be thought of in England'. She added that she not only had the other residents to think of but also the relatives, visitors and staff. That same evening before she went off duty, she sat with the couple concerned, at a dining table, opened a bottle of sherry and toasted them. This response to them was in stark contrast to having their hands unclasped by a member of staff, but was not of any help to the staff, who wanted guidelines. Sexuality was seen to be both sensitive and threaten-ing. Sexual expression was also directed at staff by some male residents and noted by them to be a sign of sexual tension or the loss of inhibition associ-ated with dementia.

The solution that management decided upon, so that employees could 'manage' what most saw as a threatening situation, was to split the couple up permanently by taking Cecil to live on another wing. Neither Rowena nor Cecil were given any say in the matter and in this respect were both muted by the dominant group of the nursing home hierarchy as well as by the staff speaking as a voice for them. The couple had little if any contact after their move, but somewhat poignantly died within the same week of each other less than a year later.

Edwina, aged in her late eighties, knew what was happening and visited the manager's office to complain after the couple were separated. She wished to discuss the idea that a private sitting room be available for such times as a different way of addressing the situation. Pondering this together, she then talked about 'how it is to lose your life's partner/husband' and how she felt 'nothing makes up for the sexual side of life'. She said that even though she was 'old and dead down one side', she would welcome a 'kiss and cuddle

from the right man', poignantly expressing her own needs and sexual identity, which could not be addressed by virtue of the fact of living in a public
place, an institution. The domain of the public versus the private world of
older people, whether sick with dementia or other conditions, could not
easily be assessed, estimated or understood by the employees. Equally, the
manager's responses were never fully understood, while the exploitation of
one resident by another could not be measured easily within the cognitive
decline of dementia.

Less Experienced Care Assistants

On a day when one care assistant had to take the day off because her child
had a hospital appointment and there was no replacement staff member
on duty, all care assistants had to help out on that wing when their own
residents were up and dressed. On this particular day, I worked with twenty-
year-old Joanna, who said she was nervous about being observed at work
and had only worked as a care assistant for a year. I endeavoured to assure
her that I was not there 'to check up on her' and tried to put her at ease,
especially as we had begun to get to know each other during the previous
months. Other care assistants mentioned this at the end of the study, saying
they were convinced at first that management had hired me to 'spy' on the
care assistants' work!

Of two men who shared a room, one was to have a bath, so while he was
soaking himself Joanna attended to the resident sharing his room. She felt
able to multi-task in this way, otherwise the work would not be done in time.
He moaned about not being washed earlier, but Joanna calmly diffused his
hints of anger. She often asks him to 'mind' his language, as he is prone to
use obscenities. One woman, Bella, was seen as a delight to attend to by this
carer, as was Gwendolyn, who the care assistant says 'sometimes plays up'.
She was the first to be washed and dressed that day because she had been
found asleep in her chair beforehand, with her breakfast of tea and marmalade sandwiches untouched. Joanna ensured that when she was dressed and
seated in the lounge, a fresh breakfast was put in front of her, which she was
encouraged to eat. Also, if very busy, Joanna pointed out that someone who
had left breakfast uneaten would be given a cold drink and biscuit, which
would suffice until the coffee was served. While in the room Bella shared,
Joanna noted that Elsie looked ill. In particular, she noticed the retraction
of her mastectomy scar, plus her cough. It was up to the care assistants to
pass this type of information on to the nurse or head of care, which the care
assistant did, also mentioning one of the men, whose breast, which is cancer-
ous, was weeping and causing concern. Elsie was due an appointment with

the consultant about her breast cancer and would be taken to the hospital for this, if well enough to travel.

One of the interesting aspects of working with this young care assistant is that she was quick to point out anything of concern and worry to her. Although she always reported these concerns to the nurse in charge, or a senior care assistant, she knew of my nursing qualifications and always wanted to discuss such things. She was constantly striving to learn and understand more about the work, and along with the other two care assistants working the day shift on that wing, she had a methodical, quietly ordered way of caring. Although none of the three women had worked as long in the job as the 'senior' care assistants on the other wing, their systematic way of doing things ensured that no aspect of the job was left undone.

Two of the day-time care assistants, who are sisters, with their mother, worked on the evening shift on a different wing to cover staff shortages. They all 'prided themselves' on the way their residents were well cared for. The overall impression of life on that wing was of a calm environment. It was something constantly observed, along with 'happiness' or 'contentment', and viewed as a phenomenon due to the layout of the wing and the historical fact of it being purpose-built, unlike the original house of the jeweller.

One care assistant had a caseload of five instead of six residents, as she said that the two men take longer than the women as they have to be shaved. When all three care assistants had finished with their residents, the two sisters and their mother, who was helping out that day, all went up to help on the wing that had a shortage of staff. This turned out to be ironic in that none of the care assistants on the wing needing help had actually taken care of an extra resident when short staffed. It is this kind of situation that quickly leads to comment and resentment, all acknowledging that the wing that was short staffed needed a more organised approach. On another day, Joanna attended to nine residents, and it was only when I called into the wing that she felt able to go for a coffee break, on the understanding that I would sit with the residents. Less experienced though she may have been, she was still able and willing to take that particularly heavy workload of nine residents to attend to all ADLs in one morning. Soon after this, however, she had time off due to ill health and upon her return told me that she and the other care assistants felt that management did not understand how their health and such a workload are closely linked and how, if they become slightly ill, it can take a while to recover.

When comparing the quiet atmosphere of two other wings to the one with its shortage of staff and regular chaos, a difference was noted, probably arising from the way they are managed. The nurse in charge of the 'chaotic' wing left halfway through the study. Of all the wings, this was the one that suffered most from a task-centred approach and a lack of cohesion and unity about what was to be undertaken in the daily tasks of caring for the residents. This wing had a higher incidence of staff sickness and was becoming increasingly more 'heavy' in the workload, with each new admission either older or frailer. Care assistants described some aspects of their work with people with dementia as 'heavy', as well as the typically 'heavy' situations of having to lift people. 'Heavy' was also used when describing having to perform most aspects of daily living, such as dressing someone and putting shoes on. This was often the case with people in severe stages of dementia. The work of a care assistant is genuinely seen to be 'heavy' and the word itself conjures up an understanding not expressed by any other word. 'Heavy' in terms of demanding; 'heavy' in terms of working against the clock to get all the morning tasks done; 'heavy' in being aware of where all their residents/patients were at any given time of the day or night; 'heavy' when management failed to recognise the workload carried daily; 'heavy' when someone died.

Lack of Skills or Lack of Thought

The description so far of the type of care given in the home involves women who care greatly in their role as care assistants, showing skills learned while on the job. This section will show work carried out in slightly different ways than those care assistants described earlier. For example, a care assistant who raised no objection to being observed at work mentioned to the deputy head of care at the end of the shift that she had enjoyed the experience! I felt she was being too kind because I had observed aspects of care that were not of the same standard as seen when working alongside other care assistants, and I would be writing about this. (Would she recognise herself in the description if ever she read the chapter, I wondered?). One resident, Nessie, who did not always want a bath, got herself up on this day and dressed herself, but the care assistant insisted that she wash and redress in clean clothes. This was seen to be a wise decision by the care assistant, as on inspection Nessie had no knickers on, just her panty hose. There were also faeces stains on her petticoat, so a clean one was put on her. Although this resident does have difficulty with many aspects of daily living, I observed Nessie showing real effort and coordination in getting it right. Would it have mattered greatly that she had no knickers on that day? She had at least dressed herself and not had to rely passively on a helper. A small stain on her undergarment could well have been tolerated for the sake of maintaining her independence. It is more than possible that what skills remain in caring for herself will erode rapidly if these tasks are consistently performed for her. While the care assistant was seen to care about the cleanliness and hygiene of the residents she was attending to, it seemed that she lacked skills and had no formal training in looking at other aspects of a person's life, such as maintaining independence. Nessie played the piano beautifully and even though she had severe dementia she was able to retain the talent needed to play, so it seemed possible that she could also be persuaded and encouraged to retain the skills needed in some aspects of activities of daily living, such as dressing herself.

This particular care assistant, who was nearing retirement, did the job reasonably well but with noticeably less thoroughness than the others. There was no indication of showing poor care to the residents, though she did appear to skip certain aspects. An example of this was not rinsing the soap off when she washed residents with flannel and soap, simply drying them off with a towel. She enthusiastically mentioned that these residents rarely get pressure sores. I observed a tendency she had of touching her face even when she had not washed her hands after attending to residents. It was this same care assistant whom I observed putting her hand into a communal biscuit tin immediately after attending to someone's underpants and pad, without first washing her hands. There are outbreaks of infection, especially urinary tract infections (UTIs), which sometimes results in confusion, immobility and mental instability. Practices such as those observed encourage the spread of infection. It is possible to place this kind of practice under the term 'ignorance in caring', rather than lack of caring, in that the intentions are well meaning but the minimal training and a basic lack of understanding affects the quality of care.

Another example of sharing their acquired skill-base concerns one man who said he felt unwell but the care assistant could not identify what was ailing him, saying that 'he was slightly fazed in the eye' and could not hold his cup, but after consultation with one experienced care assistant and the deputy head of care, his problem was identified as constipation! As his state of being 'unwell' was said not to be serious, he was promptly encouraged to sit in the lounge and wait for his lunch with a pre-lunch drink of Guinness!

Once, while accompanying a care assistant who was 'floating', she explained what that meant. Her workload that morning was to attend to two residents on each wing because of significant staff shortage. One care assistant was on a week's leave and not replaced by management, added to the shortage of staff due to sickness, meaning that the resulting heavy workload was more significant than usual. The type of attention to detail in the washing and dressing of residents carried out by the care assistants observed on other wings was not shown by this particular care assistant. Two women residents attended to were both severely disabled physically; one was not able to communicate verbally, while the other's speech was difficult to understand. One woman had spent most of her adult life in an institution known then as a mental asylum, suffering from a physical deformity. Although these two women were not the easiest to attend to, the standard of care carried out was not seen to be as good as that provided by other care assistants. For example, soap was not rinsed off before drying the person, and the clothes they were dressed in were mismatched. With this care assistant, as with some others, discussion often took place 'over' and 'above' the resident. Most of the care assistants were sensitive not to do this, but others did not seem to be aware of the dictum that this is not good for well-being. It is possible that when residents such as the two described above were being attended to, less thought was given to the issue of 'talking over' them. This is possibly because such residents are seen to be either too 'ill' or too 'demented' to know what is being said, or unable to understand. However, the need to talk in confidence within a resident's room was crucial. It was in the privacy of a resident's bedroom that the care assistants could talk quietly, sharing deep concerns. The shared work often facilitated a care assistant to voice worries to me about the kind of work undertaken, as well as the terms and conditions of employment. Most care assistants disclosed their private concerns, soliciting responses from the residents, especially women, who were keen to share vicariously in the worries about family life, for example when their children reached troublesome teenage years.

There are some care assistants who consistently let the residents know what they were doing for them and what would happen next. One care assistant who was working her notice of resignation, explained to the residents on a daily basis, face to face, during washing or dressing them, that she was 'moving on' and that someone new would take her place. She constantly assured them that the new employee would care for them in the way that she did. She was proud of the way she cared for the residents and believed the quality of her care for them was high. She, like many of her colleagues, cared enough to explain to the residents what they were doing to them. It was only rarely that one observed exasperation at having to explain again and again what was due to happen.

One qualified nurse was observed giving out medication to two women sharing a room, with no conversation taking place, including no reference to the fact that she was giving them their medicine. Working alongside her, I observed this. At the beginning of the day and upon entry to their room, the nurse neither greeted them nor explained to them why she was there. She put the tablets in the flat of their hands, folded their fingers over them and handed them a glass of water, after which they took their medicine. All this happened without words being spoken. She had previously mentioned that she was 'bored' in her work and that 'it did not appeal' to her. Trained as a nurse for two years, unlike the others who qualified many years previously, she subsequently left for another nursing job, not in the field of gerontology.

Near the end of the study, a care assistant sent by an agency on her first day of work in the home walked the length of a corridor from the area where breakfast was being served to give bread and marmalade to one of the residents in her room. She was holding the bread in the flat of her hands, not on a plate. This is where the researcher/anthropologist became nurse/advocate. It took place during the last week of the study when I undertook some shifts as nurse-in-charge, due to an extreme shortage of nursing staff. As the young care assistant was allocated to work with the nurse-in-charge, the nurse stopped giving out the medication to ask why breakfast was being handed out in this way. The most difficult aspect for the nurse-in-charge to address was that the care assistant did not actually realise that what she was doing was an unacceptable way to serve breakfast. She said she had never worked in a residential setting before and had no training in becoming part of the agency's workforce. If care in a nursing home is seen to be an extension of the way someone is cared for at home, then it is possible that this young woman did not know that what she did was unacceptable socially as well as in terms of hygiene, as it may have been acceptable practice in her own home.

This again indicates that although one may have well-meaning intentions in becoming a care assistant, an actual 'ignorance of caring' will continue to exist unless training or resistance to change is addressed. Research such as that carried out by Peace, Kellaher and Willcocks (1997) shows that despite the changes in the appearance of residential care over the years, namely in the buildings and physical environments, the personnel will remain 'resistant to change'.

Residents found the behaviour of one care assistant 'extremely unacceptable'. She had worked for a number of years in this and similar homes and was often observed cutting up a banana on a place-mat, not realising that some residents were visibly upset by it. There were side plates at the beginning of the meal but these had been taken back to the kitchen with the main dishes. The place-mats were not always wiped after meals and were often encrusted with remains of food. It could be argued that the care assistant might prepare a piece of fruit in this way in her own home.

Here the question also needs to be asked as to whether the environment of a residential nursing home actually encourages the type of practice shown here. Why did this particular young woman carry food without a plate, using her bare hands? Why did she not use a plate? Have employees become too caught up in the frenzied schedule and the imperative to get the job finished in a task-centred environment?

If, as is shown in Chapter 3 in the section on meal times, care assistants spend much of the lunch time washing dishes (in this task-focused way), then residents continue to feel isolated and neglected as staff can devote little time to them, even though assistance with eating is needed. This type of pressure at meal times discourages the care assistant from giving necessary attention to encourage a poor eater. Caregiving does not fit easily into officialdom, 'the powers that be' or establishments such as care homes. As with Foner's question in *The Caregiving Dilemma* (1994) as to whether the inevitable day-to-day pressures discourage compassionate care, the daily routine described here highlights this phenomenon.

The only male nurse, Gordon, who stressed enthusiastically that he wanted me to work with him, was said by most of the staff to be arrogant. However, in observations of him when attending to residents, such as walking with them or taking them to the toilet, he appeared always to carry out these tasks in a caring manner. Also observed was how well the relatives of the residents were able to relate to him and how they found him approachable when asking questions about their family member living there. After months of building up trust with me, he facilitated access to medical notes and many aspects of life in the nursing home, including the place in the public dining area in which to plug in a laptop computer when needed. He is a well-educated man, having been schooled by missionaries in Africa. He was undertaking a degree in health studies, having successfully completed his nursing studies before leaving Africa with his wife to settle in the UK. Care assistants and nurses invited me to eat lunch together in the garden or conservatory and, during lunch hours when Gordon was on duty, we would also take a lunch break together. He told me much about his life in Nigeria, and the kind of elite schooling and lifestyle he enjoyed as his father was a church minister. On subsequent occasions, therefore, when staff were telling me how arrogant they thought he was, I explained from my experience of working in Africa that I thought he was not actually arrogant, just that his deportment and manner were simply part of his upbringing.

Advocate though the anthropologist may have become, the care assistants, especially the older women, were all keen to listen and comment. During the study and especially since being appointed head of care, Gordon's manner with staff became more relaxed and less aloof.

Learning to Care: Acquiring Knowledge through Practice

Working with the head of care, Becky, a well-qualified nurse, showed her caring manner and quick expertise in all her dealings with residents, relatives, visitors and the care assistants. We got to know each other's life stories as we shared them with each other and the residents in her daily care. Most memorable within these conversations was her total inclusion of residents and myself in her accounts of her family life; the head of her household was undoubtedly her horse and young son. The residents often jokingly asked why her husband (a horse trainer) was always mentioned last in this named household order, to which she would reply that 'this was a different era to theirs'. This conversation took place many times, including with staff, visitors and relatives in earshot, leading to eruptions of spontaneous laughter as lives had yet again been lived vicariously and the joy of well-being experienced.

Becky, as head of care, endeavoured to bring in study days for National Vocational Qualifications (NVQs), in order to encourage the new care assistants to learn skills based on understanding and knowledge, added to the common sense skills necessary in caring for people in an institution. When NVQs and Scottish NVQs were developed in the late 1980s, it was seen to fill a perceived skills gap in many work environments, including health care. This vocational training, especially directed at people working with residents suffering from dementia, was suitable for unqualified and qualified staff, depending on their roles and competence levels. Some of the younger care assistants in the study, particularly those who had recently begun working in the home, saw this as a way of gaining qualifications as well as being equipped for the job, and showed excitement and enthusiasm at the prospect of studying. These young women had gained GCSEs at school but had neither wanted to stay on for sixth form nor been encouraged to do so by family members. At least two of these teenagers expressed the hope of gaining NVQs in order to seek entry into nursing training, so were already showing a desire to take up 'caring work' as well as be part of the 'caring profession'. In this, their choice to work as a care assistant was not random but part of a plan. Other care assistants, however, found the kind of work they undertook convenient in terms of being near home and therefore their children's schools, acknowledging that with few or no formal qualifications they had little choice in the wider job market, other than within residential care. It was these women who felt most deeply that they were 'at the mercy of the employer', especially in relation to salary and working conditions. Care assistants said that membership of a trade union was positively discouraged by management during the years of their employment.

Some of the nurses had interrupted their careers to have children and returned to work when their children were at school. As well as the convenience of location close to where they were living, these nurses also felt that this was a good way of getting back into nursing after having had a break. One nurse had worked in psychiatry within the NHS until redundancy made her seek work in the home. After a number of years working there, she sought a change in an acute unit at a hospital but returned to work at the home within two years, stating long travelling hours as the main reason for her decision. Before she moved to the hospital job, she would stress how much she wished for more opportunities to undertake courses and training days, but said she was not often able to take them up due to staff shortage in the home. She particularly felt under-valued by management and by visitors from head office, namely nursing inspectors, whom she felt were quick to criticise rather than encourage in what to her was obviously a difficult nursing job. An incident that she and others described as harsh, in which she was publicly criticised by visitors from head office, led her to apply for the new job. Although she found job satisfaction in the new work, she felt that it did not compensate for the time spent travelling by car, sometimes alone and late at night. She admits to returning to the nursing home job with a renewed vigour as well as a sense of nursing in a known situation. The residents in particular expressed their happiness on seeing a 'familiar face' return to them.

Replaceable Parts: Poor Maintenance and Supplies

Care assistants, classed as manual workers and as part of the care workforce, are susceptible to competition from the local labour market, where pay is better in local hotels than in residential care. Ironically, the main shareholder of the home under study is a hotelier. Within the nursing home as well as away from that setting, an oft-repeated phrase is, 'You get paid more to pull a pint in a pub than you do looking after a sick person'.

While working with the care assistants, in the privacy of bedrooms, discussions took place concerning such questions as the state of the linen, bedding and clothing. One said that if she saw a really threadbare sheet she would put a hole in it and place it in the rubbish bin, otherwise the sheet returned again and again from the laundry to be used on a bed. She and others felt strongly that residents should not have such poor linen on their bed, allowing the uncomfortable contours of a mattress to poke through. All care assistants despairingly mentioned that the linen and towels were thin and worn, and some of the quilts had split corners with the stuffing coming out.

Many care assistants said that the soap and bath products provided in the home were not good but 'cheap and nasty', with harsh ingredients and of an overall low quality. Supplies to make the care assistants' job much easier, such as hospital-style wet wipes for incontinence hygiene, were not always available. There were many days when the necessary incontinence pads were not available. On one wing in particular, wet wipes were always available for daily hygiene care and cupboards well stocked with supplies. This stocking up of supplies is the responsibility of the regular care assistants, so the problem of lack of supplies also involves such staff being aware of falling stock and anticipating needs. As with other aspects of the whole care programme, some care assistants seemed to manage this better than others.

The housekeeper said that emptying all the commode pots down the toilet, on a wing without a sluice, means that the contents slop and drip over the surrounds of the toilet and the floor. It is not usually cleaned immediately, as a cleaner has to be called to do it, so when a resident goes to the toilet and sits on the toilet seat, they come into contact with someone else's soiling. When a resident is brought into the toilet on a wheelchair and placed on a toilet that has not been cleaned after use by another resident or the disposal of contents of commodes, then the risk of infection is obvious. But how does one clean the commodes without a proper sluice? Even the wooden frames around the commode were in need of cleaning; pubic hair and encrusted faeces were often observed. When working on a nursing shift on that wing, I went to clean a commode but a new enthusiastic young care assistant, using gloves and disinfectant, said she 'would willingly do this more often if gloves and disinfectant were readily available'. The placing of disinfectant near toilets is prohibited because of the possibility of ingestion by a 'confused' resident. When care assistants were reminded of this, the phrase 'Health & Safety' was repeated loudly by the staff, usually with ridicule and laughter. The housekeeper and other employees pointed out that as products have childproof lids, this is a problem that could be easily overcome without the need for 'Health & Safety'.

The housekeeper also explained that all the commode pots were regularly cleaned in the bath with bleach and disinfectant. Her critical observation centred on the bleach not usually being rinsed off the bath properly before the bath is used by residents. Her worry centred on what this was doing to the skin, vulva, penis and buttocks of the residents who were placed in the bath after cleaning products had been used in this way, and the risk of cross-infection was also seen to be an issue here. Only one wing out of three has a sluice for rinsing and disinfecting commode pots. Such sluices regularly break down, resulting in the whole of the home's thirty staff being unable to disinfect the commode pots of more than seventy residents.

Included in the lack of supplies are pairs of stockings and tights, which care assistants avidly described as being 'like gold', and a real problem when they are returned from the laundry with holes in them. Many residents and relatives regularly complained about and reported the recurring loss of hosiery since admission to the home. The frequent need for items such as tights and vests being brought in for the residents by their care assistants was borne out by all staff. Some thought that even if there were increased supplies at the home, the ones the staff brought in for their residents were far superior and, if cosmetics, kinder to the skin.

During some lunch breaks, sitting in the garden with care assistants, heated discussions took place about the quality of working life. Especially mentioned was how the care assistants and nurses become sick under the pressure of what they perceive to be an increasingly 'heavy' workload. In particular, two care assistants were described as not being completely well after illness at least two months previously. One had felt awful after a bout of chickenpox but said there was never any real time to get over sickness, with a note of injustice expressed that no sick pay is given. When one of the care assistants was hit forcibly in the ribs by a woman resident, the care assistant concerned stressed that it happens with this type of job, acknowledging the real risks involved in the kind of caring that she and her colleagues readily performed. Gordon, the male nurse, on a number of occasions displayed deep scratch marks after attending to a woman resident who did not want to be helped out of bed; she in particular spat at staff, whatever their rank or position. The physical illness suffered by nurses and care assistants was compounded by the task of coping with the psychological stress of the job, while the lack of formal training exacerbates the problem.

One long-term observation concerning the staff shortage was that it was a normal occurrence for Mondays, which made many of the care assistants dread the heavier workload they would encounter on those days. When there was a shortage of staff, particularly on a Monday morning, everyone appeared to feel the pressure instantly, including residents. Staff pointed out that management did not look into the situation of more staff shortage following weekends, indicating that they felt under-valued by management, especially while endeavouring to help management find answers to problems.

In his covert study in a nursing home in the USA, Diamond (1992) shows that low-paid workers in such jobs as residential care are often seen as easily replaceable. He coined the term 'replaceable parts', which resonates with the findings here: 'the structure of labour creates a revolving door of workers, as though they were replaceable parts, while the inter-personal nature of caregiving gets systematically ignored' (Diamond 1992: 187).

Residents, too, voiced concern about the workload and turnover of staff, especially if they grew attached to a particular care assistant. One care assistant left for a job at a local veterinary laboratory, explaining that she would be paid more and have better working conditions when working with animals than with residents in a nursing home. These kinds of situations were discussed often among the staff, and did not exclude any resident, relative or visitor within earshot who wished to join in. The women residents more than the men would voice their opinions over shortages of staff and working conditions, as discussed further in Chapter 3 in the section on management.

It also appeared that the women care assistants actively engaged those women residents in conversation during their work regarding the ups and downs of family life. Women residents especially knew much about the care assistants' home background as well as those of the kitchen and cleaning staff, and often knew their children as well, who were not discouraged from visiting the home. Thus, they lived their lives vicariously through the staff and their families. In this way, they actively argued that the residential home was indeed a home from home for the resident. It can therefore be argued that the 'total institution' does not exist in the present age. That there was a constant stream of visitors, and an ease with which relatives and friends visited, is evidence of care homes not being total institutions in the way that asylums were. There are, of course, characteristics of the 'total institution' just as pervasive today, which will be discussed in the final chapter on 'creating order out of disorder'.

Creating order out of disorder is the aim of the morning's work carried out by the care assistants in the privacy of the residents' bedrooms. It was evident from the care assistants that they believe this is for the good of the resident, and such work is not for the public side of life in the lounge. Dignity was conferred upon the resident within this daily routine and its ensuing calm 'order', compared to the 'disorder of dementia' as experienced when residents such as Arthur defecated in inappropriate places including on carpets in the lounge. If, by regular routine, physical and social needs were anticipated by an intuitive care assistant identifying the wandering or pacing of dementia as illustrative of the need for the toilet, for example, then the conversion from the intimacy of the 'bedroom state' to the openly 'public space' of the lounge is deemed to be necessary.

Extended Networks: Family and Home

The care assistants built up strong networks of support and friendship among themselves, with the employees living near each other on a large housing estate in a nearby village. Few, if any, of the residents were from that housing estate but many of the parents of these workers were from the towns and villages that the residents came from, thus establishing a common geography of place, if not identity. One of the women residents, whose mother had run a public house, was well known to a number of the care assistants whose parents had used the public house, which increased mutual memories and points of conversation. As mentioned earlier, when describing the work alongside care assistants, two of them at work during the day shift are sisters, while their mother works evening shifts. One of the women laundry workers has a daughter who is a full-time care assistant. During the summer vacation from university, one female student worked as a care assistant, her mother being deputy head of care as a nurse and a member of the permanent staff. The mother-in-law of a part-time care assistant works in administration, while the male day nurse is married to one of the night nurses. The daytime charge nurse is married to one of the full-time night nurses. One of the male residents was grandfather to the cook; he died in the home at the end of the study. Another resident has a daughter-in-law who is also one of the night nurses. Well known to many people on the local housing estate was one of the care assistants and her young family. She worked night shifts at the home, so a huge sense of loss was felt in the home and much further afield when she unexpectedly died, leaving a husband, small children and grieving staff and residents in the home. This informal network concurs with other studies, where findings indicate the existence of an informal network of daughters, sisters, nieces etc. helping out and then ending up in full-time employment.

The women residents were keen to share vicariously in these networks and although none of the residents hailed from the housing estate, there were links. For example, a woman was admitted, aged well into her eighties, who had a loving attentive husband. He would visit daily and during good weather would take his wife out into the garden in a wheelchair. This involved negotiating a lip at the door's edge, so we would do it together. On these afternoons, he would tell me something of his past life as well as the present, which included saying that one of his granddaughters was the girlfriend of the son of the hairdresser at the home. The hairdresser also resided on the local housing estate. Visitors occasionally met who had mutual workplaces, of which the most interesting and extensive was the MG sports car factory. It was noted, however, that the biographies of the women residents were generally less well known than those of the men. A number of men in the home responded to photographs that the maintenance man brought in, showing the factory before it was closed. Word of this MG involvement spread, and visitors began to make contact with the retired workers in the home when they visited. This is depicted more fully in Chapter 4 in the section on activities. However, where the women would share vicariously in the care assistants' lives and families, the men had a different biography to share, usually that of common workplace interest. This particular shared biography of the men, including the grandfather of the cook, in the history of the car factory was nostalgic and always aroused interest among other visitors.

That the maintenance worker knew that the researcher enjoyed sports cars possibly added to the subject being aired. Evers (1981) found that nurses knew more about men in her study than they did of the women patients:

> However, 'Pop' tended to be a person with his individuality grounded in his own past life and contributions. Many of the nurses knew quite a lot about Pop's biography … In contrast, Gran was either divorced from her past or her past simply was not known by the nurses. (Evers 1981: 120)

However, care assistants who had looked after a resident for a number of years knew the family history well, especially if they had lived in a nearby town. These particular care assistants were the ones who took an interest in the resident and knew the families. This was not always the case, especially when the staff member was new to the work and care plans cited little of the biography of the person concerned. When the head of care introduced a written profile of the history of each resident, the resident would present not just as having dementia, but, for instance, as a multi-skilled member of various communities who happened to also be a mother of four, widowed and whose children had moved away. When resident profiles were introduced, we found out that a woman had been a publican at an inn where now stands a roundabout bearing the name of the former inn. That her mother had been the publican before her at the same inn caused much discussion between local residents and their relatives.

Many of the women care assistants showed real concern about the residents in their charge and the daily work of 'caring' highlighted in this chapter. However, without formal training or ability, it is probable that not all care assistants were able do the job of 'caring for' the resident, or even 'caring about' the resident. This is evident from the examples of the untrained agency care assistant with no experience of working in an institution, who carried the toast in her hand, and the nurse who gave the morning medication to the two women sharing a room, without a word of greeting or conversation, evidencing her lack of interest in them and lack of 'care about' them as individuals. It was enough that her paid work to 'care for' or nurse them meant that (for her) it was sufficient that the transaction took place, with or without dialogue. However, as seen from the ethnography, these two rather extreme examples were not the norm, but show that different types and styles of care existed among the staff.

What this chapter highlights are the daily working lives of the care assistants and, to some extent, the nurses. It centres on the circumstances encountered in caring for frail and sick women and men, namely society's older people. This daily work of caring includes the overwhelming smell of a pad full of faeces and urine, or a situation as extreme as that of the contents of a commode slopping onto the shoe or leg of the care assistant. These are the harsh practical issues of care work, added to the stress of caring for someone in the days and hours before death. Of consideration here is the almost impenetrable world of a person suffering from the severe stages of dementia, and the daily endeavour by staff to communicate verbally, as well as via other methods such as by tactile touching and smiling. That their job is often described by the care assistants as 'heavy' and emotionally draining in no way detracts from the quality of care provided and the relationship between care assistants and residents. This research finds that although the term 'caring' in itself is hard to define, the work involves the establishment of a continued and sustained relationship with the person being cared for, usually ill and frail, as well as with other people within the extended network of the nursing home, the 'non-total institution' within the broader community and society at large.

The rural location of this 'home from home', with its grounds leading down to the River Thames, situated off a main road in a somewhat isolated hamlet with no shops, one farm, one public house, some bungalows and large houses, can be seen to be socially isolated if not geographically remote. This chapter shows the in-depth care undertaken daily inside the home with its felt isolation by the residents, while the care assistants in particular endeavoured to bring the outside world to them, enabling them to live vicariously through the lives of the care home staff.

Chapter 3
SOCIAL ORGANISATION WITHIN THE NURSING HOME

> A senior citizen is one who was born before television, frozen foods, credit
> cards, ball point pens, penicillin, plastic, videos, frisbees, split atoms, laser
> beams and the pill. We thought a 'big mac' an oversize overcoat, grass was
> something for mowing and pot was something one cooked in. So although our
> generation cannot set the video recorder we did put man on the moon and are
> a hardy bunch when you think of how the world has changed and the adjust-
> ments we have had to make.
> —Anon. on nursing home notice board

The way in which the term 'social organisation' is used here concerns the different activities and relationships that are a feature of daily life within the home. That these are performed in public gives them a social context, acted out daily as a role and often as routine. Many of these roles are connected with other people, one-time strangers until this shared stage of life, lived in public view in the nursing home. The term 'social organisation' is useful in the setting of an institution such as a nursing home. Specific aspects of social organisation discussed in this chapter concern meal times in the nursing home, the absence or presence of religion and the style of senior management.

The Mayhem of Meal Times

Important areas of daily observation within the study were meal times. The level of activity involved, and the ensuing social interaction, was probably at its most intense during meal times compared to other times of the day. The only other activity of the day that generated so much action, as compared to the inactivity of sitting for many hours, was the morning routine of washing and dressing, or the evening one of retiring for the night. Much more social interaction took place between the residents and staff, as well as between fellow residents, at meal times, with the potential to be meaningful. At any given lunch time, six care assistants plus two nurses and two kitchen staff were involved with serving the meal, feeding people and helping to cut up food. Most notable within the activity generated by meal times and the 'noise factor' present was the amount of conversation, sometimes at shouting volume, that took place.

Although the nutritional status of older people is well documented (Dickinson and Kendall 1996), less is known about eating behaviour within care/nursing homes, and where, significantly, malnutrition has been observed. During the course of my observations, it was noted that the provision of sufficient nutrition was at times a problem. One woman who had a history of 'eating problems', as defined by her GP, seemed to exist for months on soft foods such as ice cream, and even that was often regurgitated and not swallowed. She was suffering from dementia, always seemed content and did not appear to be in pain, but consistently refused food. My field notes describe an occasion where 'I fed Maisie less than a quarter of a cup of mushroom soup which was tolerated only with spitting back the mushrooms, so that a frugal amount was taken. The ice cream was only swallowed because it was left to melt totally'. The choice for lunch had been fish fingers or sausage rolls, neither of which Maisie could manage to eat. The care assistants in their concern for her eating habits describe her as 'thin as a bird'. Another entry in my field notes, four weeks after trying to encourage Maisie to eat, states that she was 'eating and drinking much less than normal, which was never more than a mouthful anyway and looks thin, anorexic even, but never complains often just sitting and smiling for most of the day'. The days on which sausages were served always resulted in many complaints from the more vocal residents, who found them to be overcooked and hard. Residents such as Maisie did not manage to eat them, and often refused them. Residents who were unable to communicate verbally about what they liked or disliked expressed their distaste by simply not eating. A similar reaction was found when curry was served. Fish fingers became a regular feature at lunch times, after the ban on the serving of beef due to the BSE/CJD crisis (which will be discussed in the next section). Monday was often the day of choice for fish fingers, as it was for curry, which would use up left-over meat from the Sunday's dinner.

Some of the most important individual habits we enjoy as human beings are the likes and dislikes associated with food, eating and drinking. Just as in Okely's description of women in her study in rural France (1994: 53), the women in this study 'had once taken responsibility for food preparation and domestic labour'. Their family's likes and dislikes as well as their own would have been paramount, but were possibly not seen to be considered in the nursing home. Importantly, there was a felt knowledge that changing likes and dislikes were not really considered. Cheryl, diagnosed with dementia, could not verbalise how she liked to drink her coffee and was regularly given it in a feeding cup with milk and sugar. Her husband once told me that she had always enjoyed it black without sugar, so on the occasions when I prepared the drinks, she was given it this way, and she always showed her appreciation either verbally or with a relaxed sigh. It is this lack of attention to individual needs that is so evident during meal times and when drinks are served. As is seen below in the description of serving meals on one particular wing, it is the collective imperative of completing the job in a task-centred environment that prevails.

Social, cultural and environmental aspects influence eating habits. In discussing individualised care, the provision of food that residents would enjoy is significant, as vividly shown by Pru Leith in her comment cited in the introduction. It is also important to offer assistance to those needing it to eat in a safe and dignified way. The only case of obvious under-nourishment was Maisie, who often refused assistance and had a long history of being a poor eater. She and other residents made few demands to be fed by the staff, but equally may have been unable to verbalise their hunger. In this task-centred environment, her kind of individual need could be easily overlooked. Also, because Maisie seemed to be content, often just sitting quietly smiling, it is possible that she was not seen to be in need of attention. One has to remember that as Maisie had severe dementia, she was unable to express verbally what she wanted or needed.

The issue regarding adequate numbers of staff to assist at meal times is an important one. Two wings within the nursing home shared the same dining area for lunch, meaning that approximately thirty to forty people were served a meal there. On the other wing, serving thirty residents in two areas, the crockery was returned to the kitchen for washing at the end of the soup course to be used again for the dessert, as there were not enough bowls for both courses. In the large dining area serving two wings, however, the soup bowls were washed after the soup course in the sink in the dining area. The noise of cups being unloaded from a dishwasher to make room for the soup bowls rose to a crescendo in between courses. The use of members of staff for this activity was also often to the detriment of the residents who needed help and individual attention. The resultant noise and level of activity was, therefore, much louder and higher than on the other wing, especially with the involvement of two sets of care assistants and nurses waiting on the tables. Here we need to consider the shortage of staff and the kinds of tasks undertaken. Meal times could become individualised with more staff on duty, thereby ensuring adequate intake of nutrition and a pleasant social event, rather than a task-oriented procedure.

Even when staff numbers were adequate for individual attention to residents, other factors had to be considered. For example, one care assistant always preferred to sit down and feed the residents rather than fetch and carry food and crockery along the corridor to the kitchen. On a number of occasions, another care assistant insisted that the one who sat should help with the dishes rather than take a long time feeding people. A care assistant sent by the agency, and who regularly worked in the home, had completed at least two years' nursing training in the past. She was observed encouraging one resident to feed another, until a senior care assistant intervened saying it was potentially risky practice. The care assistants talked among themselves at length about this incident, highlighting the danger to the patient and their own accountability if the resident had choked on her food.

At times, when certain staff members brought the meal to the resident, they did not always note the person's sitting position and whether it was conducive to eating well and being able to feed her/himself. For instance, Rosé, who always had her meals served at an armchair on a portable table, was slumped in the chair one lunch time and told me that she was uncomfortable. I was assisting feeding another resident, so suggested to Rosé that she ask to be lifted and made comfortable when her second course was brought. Celia, the care assistant, brought the meal but Rosé did not ask her for help, nor did Celia seem to notice her position or offer to assist. Knowing that the meal would be left on the plate and taken back to the kitchen as the resident was unable to eat from such a position, I then asked Celia to assist me in making the resident comfortable, to which the care assistant readily responded.

One particularly noisy lunch time, I was feeding Cheryl, who had been shouting persistently in the conservatory at the end of the large dining area. Ivy, a shy, quiet, lucid woman, was sitting with Bob who eats appallingly and Jerry who dribbles constantly due to his clinical condition. I asked Ivy if she wished to join us for the rest of her meal at our adjoining table. She was delighted to sit with us and seemed to enjoy her meal and the company. This showed the need for more thought and planning about who is placed with whom for meals.

There were many occasions when agitated behaviour was observed, and on each occasion it could be seen to be associated with the rise in noise and conversation level, particularly when more than one discussion was going on simultaneously. It was at these most noisy times that Bob, one of the residents with dementia, would spit on the dining area floor, much to the distress of residents trying to enjoy their food nearby. The management of this behaviour was to send him back to his room. Walter, one of the male residents who lunched alone in his room, would attend the dining area at supper, sit in his wheelchair in a prominent position alone at a table and proceed to talk to anyone who would listen, in particular one care assistant, at the top of his voice. During the year of the study, I never heard or observed any employee or resident asking him to be quieter while supper was being served and eaten. A number of times a resident would complain to me about his level of speech and constant talk. During those meal times, there were few quiet moments even when Walter was eating, as he would talk while he ate!

One area where agitation was always evident was when Bob, an active resident, tried to get to his chair at a table, only to find his way blocked by the kitchen trolley, which held dishes for use at lunch and was used to take the crockery back to the kitchen afterwards. It also blocked the pathway of people trying to get past it on walking frames and with walking sticks, or in wheelchairs. This constantly caused discontent among the residents.

Environmental factors other than noise and blocked passageways were also noted at meal times, namely the lingering smell of disinfectant from a bucket used for cleaning purposes around the dining area and the smell of varnish used during the refurbishing of a resident's room. Counsel and Care (1992) and Mulley et al. (2015) offer guidelines for managers running homes and advise that they address the reduction of environmental pollution, namely offensive noise, smells and all obstacles that may cause distress, anger and frustration.

Another cause of agitation was shortage of staff in the kitchen, resulting in the late serving of food. On these occasions, residents sometimes were sitting for half an hour awaiting the first course. At one meal time, the reason given for the late lunch was that the manager was in the kitchen as acting chef because the deputy head of care, who would normally stand in for the chef, was off sick. The manager had apparently placed a whole swede in a pan to cook, so all residents had to wait for their roast chicken meal, which by the time it arrived was overdone. Later the same day, the manager was in the kitchen again making tea for visitors and social workers attending a social service review. She said that management had interviewed for kitchen staff but did not find anyone suitable, believing that the older person's dietary needs differ from what most chefs prepare. The nursing home residents want basic food rather than cordon bleu, she said. Even without being able to ascertain the manager's reasons for this, one can see an element of infantilisation in this generalisation about likes and dislikes. One woman resident, who had run a well-known star-rated hotel, may well have enjoyed cordon bleu cooking, as would Cheryl, whose husband described her to me as a fine cook, often holding dinner parties before the onset of dementia. As there was no weekend chef for a number of months, the manager was willing to work as a stand-in chef. In a discussion with the manager about the need for more staff in the kitchen, and particularly a weekend chef, she said that even advertisements in local newspapers had produced little response. It was during moments of discussion such as this that she would reiterate to me her desire for the nursing home to be a 'home from home', and her definite belief that this was the case in 'her' home, including the meals.

The Infantilisation of Meal Times

On another occasion when the manager was acting as chef in the kitchen, lunches were again late. However, agitation and annoyance increased because the sausages served were, as always, overcooked and hard. The protests from Edwina were loud and clear, but the silent protests of Sarah were noticed, as she had no dentures in at lunch time and therefore had difficulty eating the sausages. After lunch, however, it was noted that Sarah in fact had both sets of dentures in place! There were a number of other lunch times when residents would be seated at the dining table ready to eat lunch but without their dentures in place. An issue that caused vehement complaints and agitation was that of residents being given a smaller than expected portion, for instance when Edwina showed surprise one lunch time at only getting half a smoked haddock fillet instead of a whole one. She described her meal as a 'kid's portion'. As described in the introduction, the restaurateur and writer Prue Leith mentions a ninety-year-old woman who was miserable at meal times, as she was given poached eggs on wholemeal toast when she had eaten fry-ups and white bread all her life. Prue Leith gave a 'spirited defence' for the woman to choose what she wanted (Frean 1999). In the present home, one Sunday lunch time, Edwina was upset to be served 'scraps' of turkey instead of a slice or two, showing me tiny bits of turkey on her plate. Many of these women and men remembered rationing during the Second World War, and some remembered childhood and teenage years of economic depression. It was with a sense of pride that they would say how their children and husbands were always well fed in the years during and after rationing. To then find themselves in later years being served portions that they classed as less than adequate affected their dignity and self-esteem. Infantilisation can negatively influence the experiences of dependent people, in particular producing feelings of marginalisation, personal humiliation and vulnerability, as discussed by Jenny Hockey and Allison James (1993) in their chapter entitled 'Infantilization as Social Discourse'. The loss of dignity from the kind of humiliation and vulnerability that Edwina was experiencing, shown outwardly as anger, when being served a minute portion of fish or tiny scraps of turkey was conveyed to all who would listen to her.

As already mentioned, one of the greatest causes of contention was the serving up of curry or fish fingers. Upon asking the cook what the residents thought of this choice, she said that only ten or so out of seventy-five residents ordered the curry, though the staff always enjoyed it.

Considering that management always stressed to relatives and visitors that the home was the resident's home, this serving of curry clashed with that ethos. Few residents, if any, had eaten curry before entering the nursing home and few were prepared to try it. As it was something that none of the residents would serve at home, residents and relatives said it seemed a strange choice for the menu. Fish fingers were often described as 'baby food' by residents, and some residents complained bitterly. When the British beef crisis was at its height, the head office of all the nursing homes in the group decided to ban the serving of beef in any home. A number of residents felt this was an arbitrary decision, and one male resident was deeply offended. Tom, a retired farmer, reacted tearfully and angrily when served fish fingers one lunch time. He felt the residents should have at least been given the choice as to whether or not to eat beef, and certainly not served fish fingers instead. He classed fish fingers definitively as children's food, previously telling me how upset he was to be served them. Early one morning, he went missing and was found fully clothed sitting in the river in a state of hypothermia. He had to be hospitalised to recover; his stated aim was to commit suicide. The humiliation and vulnerability, as mentioned earlier in relation to Edwina being served half a piece of fish, had become apparent in Tom's demeanour even before he was found in the river. After being hospitalised, he was not re-admitted to the nursing home but transferred to another one. In discussing the infantilisation that often takes place between the carer and the person being cared for, adults state that they do not wish to be treated as infants. Relatives also acknowledge this for the person with dementia who once had cognitive function and powers.

The retired farmer, Tom, was completely lucid; he fully funded his own fees and was in control of his own finances, but felt demoralised at the insidious ways in which residents were treated as children, often by decisions of management, such as the ban on eating beef, that were then reflected in the staff's working practices. In discussing infantilisation, we need to be aware that it often arises out of the paternalism of institutional management, which can be seen to be a latent misuse of professional authority. In the context of meal times and choice of food other than 'baby food', education and training in the effects of dementia, as well as the frailty of old age, are important in ridding the staff of such paternalistic attitudes. Tom, who reacted so personally and violently, told me that by not having a choice over the serving of beef, he felt neutered. He was expressing that helplessness of institutional infantilisation which disempowers people and results in the transformation of older people into infants. This can also be seen in terms of 'mutedness', where the dominant group mutes the apparently less able. Thus, the feeling of being treated like a child in the serving of fish fingers can also be seen in terms of control, power and disempowerment. Infantilisation denies what independence remains for people, who as dependants upon others for their fulfilment of basic activities of daily living comprehend infantilising actions anyway.

The Relatives Association, a charity representing the relatives and friends of older people in homes, has suggested that the presence of relatives and friends at meal times in a residential home is beneficial to the resident, especially those with dementia. This was rarely observed in the nursing home, probably due to lack of focus on individual needs, but also due to relatives' expectations for the staff to be able to meet all the needs of the resident, often resulting from a build-up of trusting relationships.

Often noted at Sunday meal times was an overall impression of calm and peace, with little evidence of the agitated behaviour so apparent on weekdays. Calmness of approach was evident among the care staff, who all said that it was because 'management were not around'. One Sunday afternoon during the study, the lunch had been served on time. A part-time care assistant, often only at work on weekends, brought out all the meals from the kitchen on trays so that the non-experienced staff in the dining area that served two wings could get on with pouring juice, taking starter dishes away and cutting up meals. It was all done and cleared away with less noise than usual. Vi was on her own at a table, so I showed her to another table with other residents. She ate her starter of grapefruit as dessert because her roast lunch was brought to the table quickly. All the meals seemed to be speedily served and were therefore hot, notably leading to an air of contented calm. The kitchen trolley, set up for tea with a tray of doughnuts protected with cling film, was placed far away from where the residents walked or pushed their wheelchairs, so there was no agitation from people being unable to get past the trolley.

Alcohol was served only rarely, for instance at Christmas and sometimes in celebration of a birthday. Two of the male residents had cans of beer or Guinness brought in for them by relatives and were given them as a pre-lunch drink. On a number of occasions, one woman resident, Glenys, said she would have enjoyed a sherry before lunch, especially on Sundays. There did not appear to be any policy within the home concerning the serving of alcohol, and it seemed that there was an indifference to serving it rather than any strict regime in not allowing it. The serving of alcohol at any time in the home was never observed, and was said by staff to be positively discouraged by the manager, evidence again of 'muteness'. Although the manager was heard to stress her notion of 'home from home', this was not noted in respect to the inclusion of any resident in the compilation of a menu. For example, choice of what to eat was presented to residents from a list available each day, but there was no involvement of residents at the planning stages. This also shows a degree of infantilisation.

The Menace of Cross-Infection

At times, a number of residents would become sick with diarrhoea. This is always difficult to contain in an institution, but certain practices seemed to encourage its spread, for example the combination of roles played by the care assistant. These employees had the closest contact with residents, including the disposal of bodily waste such as faeces and urine from commodes and the cleaning up of residents' inappropriate defecation. During one bout of sickness from diarrhoea affecting eight residents, the cook offered to make toast and scrambled egg for all those who were sick. However, at lunch time on that day, one care assistant was observed making toast for all those who were ill and unable to leave their rooms. The offer by the cook had not been taken up. It would seem that not only was this an extra task for an extremely busy care assistant, but that she was one of the very people in close contact with the residents and, therefore, the diarrhoea bug. To be handling food as well would add to the risk of cross-infection.

Music at Meal Times

Quiet music is found to cushion and cover up environmental noise and is shown to exert a calming effect on the residents. Agitated behaviour diminishes with the playing of music at meal times, especially among people with dementia. At the end of this study, management introduced quiet music into the dining area and sitting rooms, which was seen to have a therapeutic effect on residents, both men and women, as well as staff and visitors. The Alzheimer's Society, in their recommendations for carers encouraging people with dementia to eat, advise 'a relaxed, friendly atmosphere with some soft music' (Alzheimer's Disease Society 2016). This implies that music has a calming effect in situations where aggressive or disturbed behaviour is evident, as described by Ansdell (2015) with regard to dementia and other illnesses. Visiting a residential home with his cub scout group one Christmas, Ansdell played the piano and observed a woman gently weeping. He says he realised 'that there was something interesting and important in how, although she looked sad, the music seemed good for her' (Ansdell 2015: xii).

Until the introduction of music in the home, no music was played during meal times. On the wing that served lunch to its own residents alone, the television was on, usually a news programme, constantly throughout the meal. On the wing that served people from two wings, the dining area adjoined the lounge with no partition or door. For those residents served meals from their armchairs and other residents nearby, the television set was usually on loudly while lunch and supper were served. The differences generationally between residents and employees could well account for the fact that the television was rarely turned off by a nurse or care assistant during meal times. The regular overall impression of meal times was one of rush, especially in getting each task done, and a general cacophony of sounds of crockery, cutlery and voices resulting in mayhem. Many of the care assistants who are young mothers describe serving meals to their children at home in front of the television. When new management took over in the nursing home, one of the measures instigated was a system of piped music to the three main sitting and dining areas. The positive early effects of this were immediate, but as this took place at the end of the study, long-term effects on residents at meal times and other times of the day were not noted. Garbedian's timely thesis addresses the effects of music for people with dementia living in care homes, saying that 'music may be able to reach and facilitate communication between people even when other avenues for communication may have diminished or shutdown entirely due to cognitive impairments' (2014: 124).

Making of Hot Drinks

There were many mornings and some afternoons when I would serve teas and coffees, mainly because the care assistants were so overworked and short-staffed. But it was also at these times that I was able to observe reactions from residents who wanted to make a choice of how much sugar to have in their cup of tea, for example, and the appreciation of it being hot and not spilt in the saucer before starting to drink it. The serving of morning coffee and tea at 11 a.m. and afternoon tea at 3 p.m. was over very quickly, often sloppily and with little consideration for the likes and dislikes of the person drinking. The tea was usually weak, with often only half a cup served, and a lot more sugar than the resident desired. One woman's comment was echoed by many who did not like sugar; she said that it was like drinking syrup. The large teapots in use often leaked as they were being poured, at times over the open dish containing coffee granules ready to stir into cups of hot water for the coffees. Morning coffee is served only after every resident is dressed and seated in the various lounges. The intense activity that precedes this, and the heavy workload that care assistants bear during it, contribute to the way the drinks are served. When they are so short-staffed and the care assistants have not stopped for coffee themselves, there is a real need to use another employee for this, such as a member of the kitchen staff, instead of being dependent upon a stressed workforce for the task. My role as participant researcher was welcome here in that I was available to prepare the teas and coffees for the residents when necessary. Care assistants and kitchen staff discussed a practice used in hospitals where the League of Friends prepare and hand out drinks, saying that such a home as this could do with a League of Friends to visit the residents as well as provide drinks in the busy morning shift. The perceived barrier to the implementation of such a practice was always described in a disparaging tone, using slang – 'Oh Health and Safety' – and given as an anticipated answer by the care assistants mimicking the manager.

On most mornings when serving the coffees, comments such as those of Arthur, Jim and Ivy saying how much they enjoyed coffee that morning, and especially that it was not 'slopped', showed how a well-made and well-served hot drink could provide real pleasure. It could therefore be argued that this, like the serving of meals in a peaceful environment, leads to an overall quality of life not always encountered in the home. At times when a resident needed to drink through a straw or feeding cup, it was observed how much time had to be given by the care assistant to this task, and how it often became easier to give half a cup instead of the full drink. One resident in particular, who needed help in drinking, suffering from a urinary infection and a high fever, needed regular, extra provision of drinks as part of his treatment. He was confined to bed in his room during this time. For a busy employee trying to get the tasks finished before going off duty, painstakingly offering a drink and encouraging the resident was not a priority.

Cheryl, mentioned earlier as often shouting persistently, was described to me by her husband as a 'wonderful cook and gardener' before her illness. He visited regularly and often wanted to tell me what she had been like as a person prior to illness. Since being in the nursing home and her decline from dementia, he was at times concerned that she was not able to say what her dislikes and likes were, especially regarding drink and food. As mentioned earlier, he said that she had always preferred coffee taken black with no milk and sugar, but stated that she was regularly given it in the home with milk and sugar. He pointed out the difficulty of someone attending to her who did not know her well and thus made presumptions. The care assistants found the procedure of giving a resident a hot drink cooled with milk to be quicker than waiting for a drink to cool. In a task-focused environment, this approach takes precedence over individual likes and dislikes. This is a classic example of muteness in the care of people with severe dementia. Had the care assistant paid attention to the husband's dietary requests for Cheryl, muteness would have been avoided. The decision not to pay attention to her husband's requests was the first instance of not having a voice that he encountered, and continuing to give Cheryl coffee in a form she disliked was a daily form of mutedness for her. Infantilisation and mutedness are flip sides of the same coin. For example, extra milk is added to children's drinks to cool the drinks down, and with older people enables them to drink it more quickly. Some people suffering with dementia have difficulty swallowing, so drinks were often given from a feeding cup with a lid. One woman resident, who consistently left half a feeding cup of drink or more, was well able to drink from an ordinary cup, which she seemed to enjoy and finish. However, the kind of attention needed from the carer looking after her was again unlikely to be considered a priority in the task-centred environment of 'getting the job done', even if it resulted in drinks being half drunk. Mutedness facilitates task-centred completion of the job. Furthermore, task-centred focus depends upon mutedness.

What has evolved in this section is that the kind of meal times that take place do not fit in with the concept that the manager has for the care home, namely that of it being a 'home from home'. Although a number of guides for managers and staff in residential homes emphasise the term 'home', the reality of putting this into action at meal times has to be well thought out and planned. The residents' experience of meal times is largely dependent upon how staff approach the serving of meals, as seen with Sunday lunch times, which were calmer and more relaxed compared to the bedlam of weekday meal times. Not being permitted to make a cup of tea or coffee is indicative of an institution thinking it can be all-providing. Not serving alcohol at all indicates institutionally prohibitive as well as infantilising practices. Guidelines for residential homes also highlight this, saying that 'homes may claim to be all providing but nothing can compensate for the loss of capacity to buy small goods and services or even … the stamp for a letter' (Counsel and Care 1992: 16). The loss of capacity to make a cup of tea or coffee is felt greatly by newly admitted residents to the nursing home. When that incapacity is imposed by well-meaning management, it becomes an aspect of enforced inactivity. It cannot be stressed enough what this loss of opportunity of undertaking such a routine task as tea-making means to people experiencing so many losses on admission. Add to that the diminished opportunity in deciding what to eat from a restricted menu, and one begins to see the ways in which choice and decision-making start to erode for individuals in such a setting.

There was a noticeable difference between the way care assistants conducted meal times and the more intimate jobs of bathing and dressing residents. Care assistants talked to the residents they were attending to during the process of bathing and dressing, which was not always the case when helping to feed them. This is probably due to the very nature of the task; to encourage the person to talk would be to slow down the whole process of feeding. Job satisfaction can be linked to conversation, and low levels of work satisfaction can lead to a lesser degree of conversation during such activities as meal times, washing and dressing and being helped to the lavatory. Greater work satisfaction for both resident and employee leads to important opportunities and moments for stimulation through conversation at these times. It was apparent that some of the residents in the nursing home were keen to talk in between meal courses with those sharing their table, usually no more than three people. The time they enjoyed talking with the staff was while the dishes were being removed from their tables. On the whole, the main impression was that meal times and the serving of hot drinks were not relaxed occasions in the home, but usually hectic for staff and rushed for residents.

Management

Throughout the study, and especially when working alongside the care assistants, the relationship between management and the employees was often described as tense. In particular, the interaction of the female care assistants and nurses with the female manager was always interpreted by staff as negative. For example, on a day when visitors from head office were present, one of the nurses was criticised when shampoo was found in the bathrooms. It was seen to be a poison risk, in that a person with the cognitive impairment caused by dementia could view it as a drink and ingest it. However, what the nurse objected to was the manner of criticism: loudly and in front of people, including residents. Later, while giving out medicines, the aggrieved nurse discussed the style of management with another nurse and me, especially noting the lack of constructive criticism. She stressed that most of the employees felt they were often criticised and rarely praised, even when they were doing extra work during staff shortages. She began to express a desire to look for new work, which she did, resulting in a move to a hospital job and the subsequent appointment of another nurse in her place at the home. Her stated reason to management for leaving was that she felt in need of a new challenge, whereas in private discussion she said her real reason was frustration and anger at the style of management in the home. Two years later, under new management, she returned to the home and was given more nursing and administrative responsibility within her new job description. What she and some of the care assistants expressed about management was that they felt under-valued by the manager in particular who, in their opinion, had no understanding of the kinds of tasks involved when caring for a sick older person. This was in stark contrast to the relationship built up between staff and the head of care, who constantly encouraged the care assistants and when implementing new ideas endeavoured to enable them to see reasons for change in practice and procedure as required. Two of the nurses had a similar approach when working with the care assistants, especially new and younger ones starting out in the job. Good leadership is enabling at all levels of care, especially in the role of head of care, as well as more senior management. Management should actively plan for staff training requirements, especially the need for training to care for people with dementia. This contributes to higher levels of morale among staff members, something noticeably lacking among care assistants and nurses, especially when talking about their relationship with management.

The manager's often-stated adage that the nursing home should be a 'home from home' was at times seen to be impracticable by staff. For example, no names or photographs were used on the residents' doors, resulting in the many agency and temporary staff having difficulty locating the person and the room concerned. One of the differences seen between the views of management and those of the nurses and care assistants working closely with the residents was in the interpretation of the word 'home'. The manager, a trained social worker with previous experience in the USA, often stressed to relatives and professional visitors alike that the care home was the residents' 'home from home'. In reality, this took the form of an emphasis on such details as the use of a divan bed for sick residents, instead of a nursing bed. Divans were lower than nursing beds, not normally on wheels and were more difficult for the care assistant to make up with fresh linen, as the procedure demanded more bending. When mattresses such as those to relieve pressure were needed in caring for sick residents vulnerable to pressure sores, the design of them did not fit the divan beds. The choice of pressure mattress left to the nurses and head of care included a cover that was easy to maintain hygienically when attending to residents who soiled them. However, they were not in use until suitable beds for the pressure mattresses were brought in. Nurses and the head of care wished to use rubber-fitted sheeting on the ordinary mattresses of those residents who frequently soiled them, but this too was discouraged by the manager. During the course of the year, staff morale was observed to decline until the manager left for another post. On her departure and the appointment of the head of care to the post of manager, staff morale improved greatly. What was noted by the employees as a negative style of management had been most evident during a meeting that the manager called (before she left her post) with the care assistants, laundry workers, cleaners and kitchen and maintenance staff. Care assistants and nurses informed me of the forthcoming meeting with the manager, so I was able to attend as an observer. On the day itself, the manager also invited me to attend the meeting.

Immediately I observed a confrontational approach from the manager. She started the meeting by holding up a piece of wire with much felt and dust around it, and asked if anyone could suggest what it was. A number of care assistants guessed correctly that it was the wire from the cup of a brassiere. It had apparently got caught up in the washing machine, which caused the machine to break down and incurred costly repairs. The manager asked what could be done to prevent this happening again, especially because it had put the machine out of action. After suggestions and discussion, the manager said that these wires should be taken out of the bras and staff should ask relatives to buy bras without wires in future. The decision as to who would take the wire out of each bra was taken by the manager, who said that the care assistants were to be responsible. There was evident disquiet at what was later described as extra work, but no one protested to the manager herself. The fact that bras with wires are more expensive than those without was not raised as a point of discussion, nor was there mention of consideration to those women who needed such bras.

Prompted by the manager, the discussion then centred on face flannels, which often became stained with faeces. The manager asked what the care assistants needed to prevent this happening in the future, so they suggested a return to the larger disposable wipes that used to be available for maintaining the personal hygiene of the residents but were too costly for the budget.

The manager then brought up the subject of break times for staff and wanted them to tell her what the official breaks were. She said there was some abuse of breaks, in that staff took much longer than the allotted time. She informed them that she still allowed for the opportunity of taking quick smoking breaks and said she felt she was 'being reasonable'. One care assistant responded by saying that some of the breaks affected their work, but the manager became angry and said she was not prepared to argue. However, it was observed and noted by all that it was the manager who had begun to argue, not the responding care assistant. All commented that her manner was often confrontational.

Another care assistant was singled out by name for dressing a male resident in trousers that had not been ironed. The manager emphasised that the residents 'should not look like they were dressed in a nursing home'. She suggested that the staff send clothing back to the laundry if it was not suitably laundered, pressed or mended. The manager pointed out that shabby creased clothes were unacceptable, her main reason being that there were many visitors to the home. At this point, she mentioned me by name as a regular 'visitor', saying that 'Janette's opinion is important'. I hoped that her comment would not destroy the rapport that had been built up with many of the staff, especially with the care assistants over months of working alongside each other. It also caused me to wonder what the manager really thought my purpose was in being in the home.

Discussion then centred on the smoking habits of certain residents, especially one man and his 'permission' to smoke. It was stated that his wife should have the final say in how many cigarettes he could smoke, as she wanted him to give up smoking and it was she who purchased the packets for him. He and Betty queued after coffee and meal times to get their cigarettes from the nurses' station and one nurse in particular kept them waiting and was very slow to look up from what he was doing. Where was the choice and autonomy in all this? However, at least they have their own small lounge to enjoy their cigarettes. The manager then asked the employees, and the care assistants in particular, if there were any points they wished to raise. There was no response so the meeting was closed.

The response of the employees was to seek me out regularly throughout the day, asking what I thought about the meeting, and to state how unjust they felt some of the points were. The problem of the condition of clothes returned from the laundry was more involved than the manager's suggestion that unsuitably pressed or mended clothes be returned to the laundry; a number of the care assistants explained that this was not always possible as sometimes the resident concerned had no other clean clothes available.

The senior housekeeper said there should be a more realistic smoking policy in that there should be a separate lounge designated for smokers, or the use of the conservatory, which had once been allocated to smokers. She felt that some of the visitors would stay longer if they could smoke with their relatives and had observed how, during good weather, visitors spent much more time sitting in the garden enjoying a cigarette with their relatives. However, the hairdresser previously told me about one resident who sat in the conservatory to smoke. The hairdresser told the management that she was unable to get rid of a cough, so smoking had been banned in the conservatory, which in fact led into the open hairdressing area at the end of the large dining area. It was obviously a topic of contention as other employees told me, without being prompted, what they felt about the smoking policy. All emphasised the need for a proper location for smokers.

The housekeeper then went on to discuss the staff meeting and how only she and one care assistant had made comments. She said that colleagues always felt threatened and intimidated in meetings with management, and especially that the manager was always too quick to argue, which she said most employees did not want to confront. At one time, the housekeeper worked shifts as a care assistant during staff shortages. She enjoyed the close contact with residents, but on becoming senior housekeeper she was informed by the manager that she would not be allowed to take shifts as a care assistant. She complained to me that this was a double standard as the deputy head of care worked extra shifts in the kitchen, as did the manager when the cook was away. She and some of the care assistants also explained that when the manager works in the kitchen she has nail varnish on. The staff were not allowed to wear nail varnish at work and said that there was one rule for employees and another for management. What the employees viewed as a double standard for behaviour gave rise to some of the greatest tension between management and staff. Low levels of work satisfaction have significant consequences for management, in that absenteeism becomes high and staff turnover increases, with adverse effects on residents. Workers experiencing low levels of job satisfaction often have feelings of low self-worth and ultimately the commitment to the job suffers. Although low job satisfaction affected the care assistants and nurses, staff tried to maintain a high standard of care for the residents.

Other examples of double standards, or even evidence of favouritism, were shared by staff and residents on several occasions during meal times. For example, the hairdresser said that the manager, when at work in the kitchen as cook, was offering bread rolls with the soup course to one table of four residents only. The care assistants waiting on the tables said they did not like special treatment. This was observed throughout the study and often commented upon by staff, especially temporary staff viewing it for the first time. For example, Charlotte M, a resident, is served a pot of tea on a tray every tea time, instead of the individual cups of tea as served by the care assistants. The resident concerned is lucid, not frail and able to cope with most activities of daily living by herself. This routine changed when the new management took over. The manager who left once explained that this resident was given a private room, even though her fees did not cover it. Therefore, the manager regularly let that room at a loss to the company, as the woman had no finances to pay towards the costs and no relative willing or able to do so. However, the procedure of serving tea on a tray individually to a resident, while others at the table were served tea in a cup, when changed by new management was felt to be a fairer system according to the care assistants.

After the meeting during which the manager had commented on my opinion being important, I went to speak to three care assistants individually, explaining that the study was looking at issues to do with management as well. All three care assistants said they had understood this at an early point in the study. One care assistant informed all the others when chatting in the staff room that I was there to observe all aspects of nursing home life, and 'not as a spy for management'! I felt with relief that this emphasised rapport and that an understanding of the study had been built up by then.

One positive comment concerning the present management of the nursing home was made by the deputy head of care. She said she had seen many changes working in the nursing home for eight years. The most significant help to the work of caring was made by the increasing availability of supplies, such as large wipes/swabs and incontinence pads. When she first worked in the home, there was always a great shortage of such supplies. However, she and other employees remarked that current management did not have the same contact with the residents as earlier managers, who also owned the home, running it as a small family concern. These staff mentioned that the people whom the present manager had most contact with were visitors and relatives.

Becky, the head of care, who was later appointed manager, rarely commented to me about the style of management, but did suggest that a closer working relationship was needed between management and employees such as nurses and care assistants. Her proposals were not always implemented, and she described one occasion on which she was upset with a management decision. A care assistant who had worked for years on night duty died suddenly, leaving a husband and small children. This greatly upset the staff as well as residents. All the employees knew her well, some living near her on the local housing estate. The head of care wanted to place an extra staff member on duty on the night of her death to give support for the women employees who were grieving. The manager did not deem this to be necessary and positively forbade it, denying the support that could have been so thoughtfully offered.

The head of care was consistently keen on quality of life improvements, even if things became evident that showed up weaknesses of practice and procedures. She considered that the study coincided with her perceived role in the home of raising standards of nursing care and later as manager. She always ensured that I knew of new developments such as proposed inspections by the health authority and the meeting to introduce the new management to the staff. Two of the employees offered to show me their letters from management detailing the new changes when the company decided to sell major shares in the nursing home. I asked the administrator of the home about the change in shareholders. She said that, in her opinion, it would not affect the 'on the spot' management of the home.

The new main shareholder, who had previously been a minor shareholder in the home, was a hotelier, managing a small group of hotels, with the home the only nursing home in the hotel group. One of the women residents said that relatives such as her daughter should have received letters from management at the same time as employees, but only received them days later. This resident was completely self-funded with no financial assistance from social services, and said that it would have been a common courtesy to inform every family and employee at the same time.

Key informants in the study, such as care assistants, said that what was distressing about the style of management, predominantly meaning the manager herself, was how and when she made criticisms. All were of the opinion that criticism was 'given in the heat of the moment', which often coincided with stressful times of staff shortages and especially those tender moments after the death of a well-loved resident. One example of 'heat of the moment' criticism concerned a woman resident sitting in the lounge without stockings. Her relatives had visited one morning to find her like that, whereupon the manager immediately found the nearest care assistant and criticised her for this in front of the visitors. The care assistant was not the woman's key worker, but knew that she was awaiting a dressing on a small skin nick in her shin, and explained this to the manager. Later she told me she felt most aggrieved by the manager's immediate response, without first finding the resident's key worker. The care assistant said she felt there was no control over the kind of blame attributed by the manager.

Public criticism was also observed on another occasion, while sitting with residents one morning in the open dining area, which also included space for the piano and a section for hairdressing. The manager walked quickly through the area, picked up a pair of clean stockings left on the piano and, shouting loudly, asked who had left them there. No one answered her and she went quickly down a corridor. One of the nurses sitting nearby told me conspiratorially that that was the 'kind of question we can do without', mentioning how busy that morning's work had been, and how all the care assistants on that wing had washed and dressed extra residents in order to get the work done before lunch. The nurse said that it would have been far more sympathetic for the manager to thank everyone for doing extra tasks than make what was seen to be a petty comment about tidiness, especially considering her much-repeated phrase, 'home from home'. Some care assistants told me that they felt the manager was 'only interested in smells and appearances'. For example, one resident had regularly been urinating on her bedroom carpet in the afternoons. At the end of one afternoon shift, the manager, dressed in a bright pink jacket and accompanied by the administrator, brought out a new vacuum cleaner that would clean up liquid spillage as well as dry clean.

The care assistants classed this as 'all show', whereas the manager herself said that she liked to be 'hands on' in her approach to running the nursing home. Another example of a negative comment from the manager can be seen when she found one of the residents sitting with his head down in his lap. I watched the manager telling the nurse that she thought this was wrong, but I had also previously observed how often the care assistants and nurses tried to encourage him to lift his head and look around at what was happening, but to no avail. That too took place on a day when there was staff shortage and extra work for all the staff, with no indication of thanks or praise from management. There are different interpretations here about what it means to be a manager, especially the expectations of praise when earned by the workforce.

The nurse who moved to a hospital nursing job wanted to talk with me about attitudes of management, giving as a recent example the account of the death of one resident. The woman had been living in the home for two years, was very ill all the time and had therefore received a lot of attention from care assistants and nurses who felt very close to her and her family. Within half an hour of the undertaker taking the body away, the manager telephoned to say that someone was going to view the room. What upset the nurse was that the dead resident's belongings were still in the room, despite the previous arrangement that staff and family would clear them the following day. The nurse was in tears when relating this incident, saying that she felt the dead woman had somehow been violated.

One area in which the care assistants and nursing staff said that management did not listen to the 'grass-roots level' was that of staff shortages, especially during shifts when one person or more was off sick. No extra pay was offered for carrying the additional caseload when on duty. Two nurses related to me how they made a tally of the shifts of one particular weekend. Thirteen shifts in total had not been covered, which in reality meant staff taking on the care of extra residents. How the staff shortage was seen in practice is given in this example. On Saturday between 8 a.m. and 1 p.m., the home was three staff members short; during the 2–5 p.m. shift, two staff members short; between 5 and 9 p.m., one staff member short; and for the night shift, 9 p.m.–8 a.m., one staff member short. The following day, the morning shift was two staff members short, and the afternoon and evening shifts were both also two members short.

Administrative and nursing staff knew beforehand about the coming staff shortages as staff were away on holidays, but only on the Friday was a telephone call to the agency made to say that five care assistants were needed to cover the weekend shifts. The residents started to comment more frequently about the shortages of staff during the course of the study, especially if it affected them, such as not being able to have a bath. Near the end of the research, one resident said that 'there was a constant feeling of shortage of staff and rush to get things done before shifts ended'. All opportunities for discussion centred on the constant theme of members of staff leaving and the feeling that staff members were not valued by management. The resultant morale for both residents and staff members was low. One of the youngest care assistants returned from a tea break in the staff room one day saying that what was needed was a 'mass staff walkout'. She said that only then would management 'sit up and take note' of the workload, staff shortages and stress of the job. She said that even though the manager often mentioned that the door to her office was always open and that staff could go in and 'talk about anything', more often than not she was busy with a visitor or someone else in the office. What this shows is that the manager was seen to be unavailable, even if in reality this was not the case. On another shift, a young care assistant attended to fourteen residents getting up in the morning. Upon hearing criticism from the manager about something she described as 'petty', she answered the manager back, much to the delight of other staff members. This young woman was upset because she felt there was never any praise from management, only criticism. A number of staff told me that they were cynical about staff shortages not being met, because on the days of inspections by authorities, staff numbers were always complete. On one inspection day, the home was observed to be fully staffed, whereas the following day there was a staff shortage with two care assistants missing.

One care assistant who had two weeks off sick said that she 'had lost a lot of money', meaning that she did not get paid while off sick. She and other care assistants stated that this was unfair management practice as often the reason for being off sick was their work in the nursing home, with susceptibility to infection and the physical strain of lifting patients, sometimes without the aid of a hoist. One of the nurses said that the style of management, which she described as being 'on the defensive', resulted in staff thinking they could not negotiate with management about such issues as sick pay. Membership of a trade union had always been discouraged, so the care assistants had become used to not having a forum for such issues as the non-payment of sick pay. Some of them tried to explain to the manager, to no avail, that they often became sick because of working in that environment and because of the type of work involved.

The male nurse at the nursing home also voiced some concerns to me about the style of management. He had his faxes from Africa intercepted by administration and there was a delay in receiving them. He said that they were only sent by his family twice during family emergencies, and yet each time it had taken a week for them to be given to him. He described this as petty management by the administrator, whom he thought had reported him to the manager for 'sitting in the office while everyone else was working'. He told me that he was in fact sitting at the nurses' station on those occasions writing up his nursing notes. He was distressed as to why a staff member had gone to the manager about him, without first finding out the real situation. He laughed as he described the manager arriving to reprimand him, only to find that he was working! The sadness of the situation, he said, was that as a senior nurse he should not have had such an uneasy working relationship with management.

At times, some residents expressed the thought that management had no real understanding of what life was like living in the home. One afternoon,

Edwina told me that at a residents' meeting she had brought up with the manager the issue of the constant heat in the main lounge, as two residents refused to have the window or door open, even on a summer's day. The manager apparently replied to Edwina that she had her own room to sit in if she wished to have the window or door open. However, Edwina explained to me that she preferred company in the lounge during the day, rather than sitting alone. It would seem that very little can be negotiated with the manager, who, as previously mentioned, used the same style with the staff, ultimately leading to low morale. There were a number of occasions when I specifically tried to engage the manager in discussion about her perspective on the running of the home. This turned out to be difficult as she always turned the conversation around to discuss her training and work as a social worker in the USA and the kind of perspectives on ageing that she says were different from the UK. There were times when I was compelled to act as advocate for the care assistants, but this was only possible with the head of care and not the manager. Discussion with the manager concerning the dissatisfaction of some residents with her managerial style was never possible as she was quick to change such subjects of conversation.

Modern Management

When the staff met the new managers of the nursing home, one care assistant employed temporarily acted as a spokeswoman for the staff by asking whether a pay increase would be considered. The other staff described her as 'quite brave', as few employees spoke up at meetings. She had mentioned the heavy workload of care assistants within the nursing home at a meeting for regular staff, pointing out that of all the nursing homes she had worked in, this nursing home had the 'heaviest workload'. At the same meeting with the new administrators, the staff members were told that the care home manager was also leaving. Two of the care assistants said after the meeting with the new management that they were convinced that only residents were important to the management, and not employees. They said that they felt any changes would be about 'getting more money in from social services and private residents'. During the meeting, the new management had addressed the issue of shortages by asking the staff to encourage their friends to apply for work in the nursing home. One care assistant had challenged this by saying that she would not do this to her friends as 'it is not a good place to work'. She also pointed out the poor wages, which must have been noted by the new managers as a pay increase was implemented within two months of the changeover.

In the days after the meeting with the new management, different staff members told me that they felt they could approach them with ideas, and especially areas for repairs and much-needed supplies. The housekeeper told the new managers that another domestic should be employed, especially during the day, as the carpets were not being cleaned as often as she thought necessary. Another member of staff reported the faulty switch on the television, which resulted in the volume always being much louder than desired. Some staff members told the managers about this at the same time as discussing the need for a ramp from the conservatory to the garden, which had been suggested two years previously. Another area of concern for both residents and staff was the need to have all en-suite bathroom doorways widened to allow room for wheelchair access and turning. This would greatly relieve pressure on the few communal baths and pacify the residents who paid extra fees for this facility in their rooms and were not able to use the bathrooms and toilets concerned. The housekeeper, on being asked by management what she most wanted in her work, expressed the wish for a different cleaning supply, as the present supplies did not clean well enough. She also said that the odour of the cleaning materials currently in use was unpleasant, and that there were other more suitable supplies on the market. The morale of the staff began to improve as some of these suggestions were quickly implemented, the first one being the construction of the ramp to the garden for ease of access for people with wheelchairs and those using walking sticks. The difference between trying to negotiate steps with a walking stick and using a ramp was noticeable for the residents concerned, and enhanced their quality of life.

Some care assistants said that the temporary care assistant who had asked at the meeting for better pay and conditions had not received any shifts in the weeks following the meeting. She was given work only when the home was so short-staffed that no one but her could be found to fill a shift at short notice. Within two weeks of the meeting with new management, this was altered in her favour. The only applicant for the advertised vacancies was a seventeen-year-old female. At one time during the study, the head of care had been adamant about not employing seventeen-year-olds as care assistants, but the need was so great that she was employed, on the understanding that she start NVQ training immediately. Interestingly, she fitted in well with the staff, and got much guidance from senior workers on how to do the job. For a number of years, there had been a difference in the amount paid to care assistants on the same evening shift. Some of these hours are classed as unsociable, yet not all the staff received the extra pay for unsociable hours under the old management. This was another discrepancy sorted out early on by new management, and did much to raise the morale of those on the evening shift.

Among the staff, and the care assistants in particular, there was a noticeable rise in morale after meeting with the new management. The care assistants regularly expressed their feelings of not being appreciated by the previous manager, and the nurse who sought work elsewhere after being criticised publicly often commented on how the manager's style should have been less confrontational. She and other staff members felt that the combative style constantly undermined their best endeavours for the residents, as well as undermining their efforts to improve their own practice. Upon negotiating with the new management, the staff commented upon the difference in style and how these new managers were prepared to listen to them as individuals as well as a group. All staff, including the kitchen and maintenance staff, hoped that this style of management would last into the future. Although it was not possible to observe for any length of time the style of the new management, there was an impression of openness with both staff and residents about issues to do with the home. Most significantly, the construction of the ramp from the conservatory to the garden was an early indication of how the new management would respond to the stated and perceived needs of both the staff members and the residents. Access to the garden became easier, and with it a toing and froing of residents, their relatives and staff, allowing them to spend time in the outdoors and experience a special aspect of quality of life outside the institution's walls.

Chapter 4
MANAGING ACTIVITIES FOR THE RESIDENTS

Man finds nothing so intolerable as to be in a state of complete rest, without passions, without occupation, without diversion, without effort. Then he feels his nullity, loneliness, inadequacy, dependence, helplessness, emptiness.
—Blaise Pascal (1623–1662)

Against boredom the gods themselves fight in vain.
—Friedrich Nietzsche (1844–1900)

When describing daily life as lived in the home, the word that residents used regularly was 'boredom'. Frail residents described hours of inactivity as extremely monotonous and frustrating. They also described their daily lives as tedious, uninteresting, with every day being the same as the next. Some residents had lived for five years or more in the home, and apart from the provision of activities felt there was little with which to occupy themselves. One of the features of the care home highlighted by management when showing relatives or proposed residents around was the emphasis on week-day activities with an occupational therapist. The activities were conducted by a young woman who had graduated with a history degree and then taken up work at the nursing home on five afternoons each week. She was enthusiastic, creative and much loved by the residents. Her diverse activities for these residents included craft-making, which incorporated the seasons, for example the making of Easter bonnets and items for the summer fair and Christmas holiday. Other activities involved exercise for immobile people, conducted while sitting in chairs, and quiz sessions.

Within a few weeks of the study beginning, the activities leader gave notice of resignation, as she was expecting her first baby. Management duly advertised and appointed a woman who had trained as an occupational therapist, returning to work from a twenty-year break. It was interesting to observe the dynamics and process of the afternoons when the activities person was present and what emerged as a pattern for these afternoons. There was great expectation on the part of the residents, followed by much aimlessness and despair when they began to see the change of style and emphasis. Afternoons buzzing with life and activity changed to passive hours filled with inactivity, when, for example, the activities leader often grouped residents of her choice around a dining table and read their horoscopes from the daily newspaper. Residents told me that this would be acceptable occasionally but not as a regular feature. She was observed on many occasions relating family events to the group, who could not and did not respond reciprocally with similar stories, as most had long outlived their family members. The way in which she chose a resident for these activities, usually involving a group of participants around a dining table, appeared to depend on a resident's ability to communicate with her. The manager, on becoming aware of this, asked her to consider 'one to one' work with people with dementia, and other residents who may benefit from such an approach, but this was not seen to be carried out. She was asked by the manager to try activities with people with dementia, such as washing the crockery after afternoon tea, or supervising the making of a pot of tea with certain residents, but this too was not undertaken.

A regular weekly fixture was the bingo session conducted by a woman whose mother had been a resident until her death at the age of 100. This woman, Moira, was of an extrovert personality and was well known to the residents, each of whom she knew by name. There was always a large group of residents for this particular activity, and employees too were enthusiastic for this event, commenting on how the participants were all animated afterwards. Moira was also an accomplished singer of popular songs and joined a pianist on at least one occasion to conduct a 'sing-along' of well-known songs with the residents. Another pianist had been visiting the home every few months for many years, for an afternoon of singing, which was always well appreciated by the residents, including those with dementia, who would often sing along word perfect.

During these musical afternoons, this woman pianist played many songs that the residents knew well, and on every occasion one woman with dementia was observed standing and singing all the words with gusto. One of the men mouthed all the words without actually singing, while many of the residents' faces expressed how much they were enjoying themselves, even if they were not actually singing the songs. Three women in the lounge off the communal area where the piano was located were content to listen from afar. One resident with dementia got up from her chair to thank the pianist after every song, while another of the residents constantly told her to sit down! The face of Dora getting up to say her thanks was so expressive, full of understanding of what was being sung. The pianist asked for requests, and one woman with dementia requested a hymn, which many residents sang from memory. Tea is normally served after 3 p.m., but the activities leader interrupted one afternoon session to make tea and serve it at 2.35 p.m., just thirty minutes after the music had started. This caused much unrest among the participants, while some care assistants wondered why it was cut short when most people were still singing heartily, including the pianist and staff. The activities leader was cajoled by residents and staff into delaying tea so that the music session could continue.

After tea, the pianist played again and more people with dementia were seen to be singing along with the melody, often remembering all the words. Cheryl, suffering with dementia and often shouting due to her inability to communicate verbally, was seated alone in her room while the singing was taking place, having been left there by the care assistants, who said that her shouting would be disruptive. The music could be heard from her room and staff noted that she was calmer, despite being alone. Another woman, whom the care assistants describe as being obsessive in her repeated requests for the use of the toilet, chose not to participate in the musical afternoon, but had to be pushed in her wheelchair through the gathering so as to be taken to the lavatory. One of the women mumbled to herself the whole time the pianist was playing, but did not seem to disturb the other participants.

These afternoons represented some of the most enjoyable times for both residents and staff. If one could measure quality of life, this kind of afternoon could be seen to contribute greatly to a contentment, happiness and exuberance that was rarely seen on other occasions. A number of the residents said that it was a good reminder of their past. For some of the women, the songs reminded them of times before they were married, when they had much freedom working in munitions factories or on the land during the Second World War. To see the same joy and contentment on the faces of both men and women suffering with dementia enables one to see the communicating power of music. Observing Dora trying to get up and thank the pianist after every song shows the benefit of reminiscence therapy with people such as her in that environment. Dora, in particular, as with other residents with dementia, responded to being with a group of people sharing in a pleasurable and stimulating activity and thereby relieving the tedium of the other afternoons, of which there were many. Studies such as those by Denney (1997) describe how agitation is seen to decrease when soothing music is played. This was well observed in Dora, Sarah and others with dementia, who were content and peaceful long after the community singing had ended. Interestingly, the meetings run on occasional Saturday afternoons by an evangelical group did not have the same calming effect, probably because they were interspersed with readings and talk. These meetings are looked at in a brief section on religion at the end of this chapter. The afternoons of community singing were also occasionally conducted by Moira, who not only was a good singer but extrovert in personality and in tune with what the residents wanted. These musical afternoons show how vital it is to residents and staff to have well thought out activities, and especially for the participants to be able to express their inner selves through songs known to them. Their previous lives were of much significance to them during these afternoons, when songs associated with their past became a reality once more. Many of the usually quiet residents were seen to be animated in the hours following these singing sessions. The joy of communion with others was evident, and this together with the songs and their retrieved memories proved to have a lasting effect.

Excursions and Outings

During the year there were six outings for the residents. One outing that took place in early autumn was a trip to a park run by a wildlife trust. Twelve residents went along, with an equal number of helpers, including three daughters of residents. One daughter helped even though her mother was unable to come due to extreme frailty. The former help of a resident also went even though the resident himself was unable to go. The husband of a care assistant, the male partner of the activities leader, plus the manager and head of care were all allocated one resident each. Care assistants were dismissive of helping out on the day trip as they would have had to take a day off to do so. They stated strongly that outings should be classed as working days and opportunities to go during the year should be given to all care assistants wanting to do so. Management were just as unrelenting in their idea that a day off should be given up by the care assistants who wished to help.

The bus hired to take the residents on outings is a large, old and ugly-looking vehicle with the name of a town on the side followed by the words 'disabled' in huge letters. All except one resident were pushed in wheelchairs to the coach, performed without hurry by the attendants. The driver ensured that all the travellers were secure in their seats by the fastening of seat belts. There was space for wheelchairs to be fastened to avoid having to lift people in and out of seats. The only woman pedestrian, who became tired during the trip, could well have used a wheelchair for some time during the outing.

The cook had packed a picnic lunch, which was eaten in the outside seating area near the cafe. Many of the residents ate more vigorously than usual, and cups of tea were bought from the cafe. The woman I accompanied has poor vision but from her wheelchair she was able to view closely the exotic birds such as South American macaws, ducks and swans, as well as many other animals, including Peking bantam cocks and a Vietnamese low-bellied hog with its two young. All the day trippers and helpers seemed really pleased with the venue, especially the ten-minute miniature train ride around the park, waving to onlookers as they went.

Another outing was arranged for late November in order to provide an opportunity for some of the residents to do some Christmas shopping. The shopping centre chosen was to be Milton Keynes, as it is spacious, under cover and has easy access and facilities for wheelchairs. However, on the morning of the trip the bus did not turn up, so the consensus of opinion was for a trip to a large garden centre in the Cotswolds instead. It was a pleasant drive through scenic countryside, with the residents and helpers travelling in private cars. The car I travelled in carried a resident who had been an enthusiastic cyclist in his youth along with his wife. He knew all the villages we passed through and gave us map references and points of interest, and was especially animated when being driven through a scenic valley. The only time I had observed the kind of enthusiasm he was showing was when he described his cycling days during occasional conversations. Some of the residents bought gifts to give to family and friends at Christmas, while all carefully perused the produce on sale. One resident with poor vision was wheeled in her wheelchair up close to each item that she wanted to see. A meal was chosen by everyone in the group from the menu in the cafe at the garden centre. The residents who do not usually eat much food at meal times said they really enjoyed the meal, including 'different' food such as lasagne, some managing much bigger portions than normal.

A summer trip billed as an outing to a town on the River Thames caused much excited anticipation for the residents. All were on board the coach by 2 p.m. and returned two hours later. Two women seated on the long seat at the back of the coach were not able to communicate very well verbally; one, Jessie, suffered from dementia, and the other, Nora, had been institution-alised in a psychiatric hospital for thirty years. Though not verbally com-municating, they were completely at ease in each other's company. Moira, the volunteer helper who ran the bingo sessions and whose mother had lived and died in the nursing home, sat with them. On the next seats sat Vicky, who suffered with dementia, and Katherine, who had a habit of shouting incessantly. One of the helpers asked me to sit on the seat across the aisle from them. Benjamin, who rarely conversed, and Nanette were seated indi-vidually. Nanette had spent many years in a psychiatric hospital and always enjoyed outings. Helen and Cecil were seated individually, while Bella and Dora, both suffering from dementia, sat quietly together. Vi was happy to sit quietly alone, while Sarah and Gwyneth, also dementia sufferers, sat peace-fully together. Hanks, another dementia sufferer, was seated alone as he had a tendency to become agitated and sexually provocative. Millie also sat alone. Rose and Amy were seated together, and Len sat enthusiastically near a window in his wheelchair. Ethel, who had also spent many years as a patient in a psychiatric hospital, managed to sit in a coach seat, and like Rosalind was thrilled at the prospect of the trip. Rosalind had spent all her life in an institution, having had an illegitimate child when young and unmarried, the outcome of which was a court ruling that she be sent to an institution, where she remained until admission to the nursing home. The activities person and the male nurse-in-charge sat at the front of the coach.

This was a day out for the not so able-bodied, which included people with dementia. However, Isabel, on reading the sign on the outside of the back of the bus saying 'disabled', read it out and promptly said, 'But I'm not disabled'. Someone answered that it was meant for the 'wobbly' as well; she readily agreed to being 'wobbly'. When climbing up the steps of the bus, Isabel was asked if she could manage it alone, to which she replied, 'Yes, I'm all growed up now', showing her sense of fun. Usually a quiet woman, she was encouraged to continue to talk and joked about Sunday School trips to the seaside. Katherine whined incessantly about where we were going and how long it would take to get home. The nurse-in-charge would not get involved in trying to pacify the woman who was moaning, and left it to the volunteers to try and quieten her. One of the helpers eventually insisted that he and the activities leader come and talk to Katherine. It appeared that the leaders of the trip were happy to sit at the front of the coach and leave the volunteers to try and keep the participants content.

When the coach arrived at the town, the driver turned away from the direction of the river, which meant he was not going to drive within sight of it. This caused much consternation among the volunteer helpers, who were sad that the activities person had not seen the need to plan the coach route via the river, which many of the passengers would have known and remembered. The helpers and the care assistants in the planning stage at the home all thought that the picnic would be eaten within sight, sound and smell of the river. Instead, the chosen venue for the picnic was a lay-by along a main road that had road equipment, builders' bricks and sand in it, as well as road labourers themselves in vehicles going back and forth. Everyone ate the picnic food on the bus parked in the lay-by. The drive had passed some country public houses with large car parks, so that with some planning, prior permission could have been obtained to stop for drinks. One of the helpers said that if she had known what was going to happen, she would have bought all the trippers a drink in a pub herself, rather than sit in a lay-by. On parking in the lay-by, Moira, one of the helpers, said 'How awful, it's as though they are to be hidden away, what a crying shame!' The drive afterwards was picturesque, but the coach was airless until a request was made for a door or roof slat to be opened. Otherwise there would have been no breeze felt or smells from the countryside. Benjamin kept his head up all the time, intent on seeing everything, and was very chirpy. After the picnic, he continued to look out of the window constantly, whereas in the home, at any time of day, he is often to be found with his head in his lap or on the table. Rose articulated the thoughts from childhood that she did not want the day to end.

The aftermath of such events is the shared memory of the participants and the opportunity for continued conversation about the day at various times in the future. However, on the days after various trips out of the home, little or no reference to the outings was made by the activities leader. Care assistants keen to hear about the days' events would converse with the residents about their experiences of such outings, and were keen to ask the helpers, including myself, about the days out. It would seem that an outing is a good topic of conversation for the participants to be encouraged to participate in afterwards, thereby stimulating remembrance of happy events. Flo, in particular, was always keen to relate her enjoyment of the outing over the days to follow. When considering reminiscence therapy, as mentioned earlier, these outings can be seen to link with residents' past lives. As with the musical afternoons, these types of activities can encourage expression of past lives in ways people value. The despair felt by the helpers over the badly planned picnic on the river trip was due to the fact that it seemed to give some indication of the worth or value that was placed on the residents as people by the occupational activities person.

An outing was arranged to visit a rainforest. On the day concerned, after the group had left, one resident was found to be quite upset at not having been able to go on the trip. Later in the day, her anger was especially directed at the activities leader, who said that she would take her out in her own car in the near future. Most of the decisions regarding who goes out on outings appear to lie with the activities person, though, at times, care assistants have protested about someone not being included, who was then able to go. The outing to the rainforest was not seen to be successful, as there was no cafe to take the residents to for a cup of tea and the owner of the rainforest was not pleased with wheelchairs, saying his paths of wood chippings would not be suitable. Some of the care assistants were quick to point out that with better planning this particular venue could have been avoided, and that this was yet another indication of the activities leader's lack of organisational ability.

The resident who was upset at missing the trip was driven by the occupational activities person to a garden centre on the Sunday afterwards. Here the resident bought a plant for her key worker and was pleased with her time out. The activities person later informed me that as she had taken time on a Sunday to do this, she would claim time off from a weekday, which would ultimately mean that many residents would be deprived of an activity session on the day concerned. This seems in stark contrast to what care assistants were allowed to do for outings. If a care assistant wished to accompany residents on a trip, management stressed that she could only do so by taking a day off, which in effect meant working one day for no pay, so the staff very rarely helped out on these trips. It was this kind of management decision-making that ensured staff felt under-valued in their jobs and as human beings.

Afternoons without the Occupational Therapist

Even on the afternoons when the occupational therapist was away on holiday, off sick or on a day off, it was evident that the residents looked forward to the activities, despite commenting that the session had not been stimulating and was even boring. For the person taking part, the anticipation and expectation in the half hour beforehand was an important part of the stimulus. It was for this reason, and to give light relief from the constantly burning television, even while no one was seated in the lounge, that I was asked to hold an activities session. The care assistants and head of care were unanimous in their opinion that 'somebody should do something' and felt that as the week included Valentine's Day, the activity session should be centred around that.

People who did not attend activities sessions were invited, as well as the regular attendees. One idea from the care assistants involved the planned participation of people with dementia, so some were included in the event. The activity chosen was an alliteration game around the phrase 'Valentine's Day'. All the letters in that phrase were outlined down the side of a large poster-size card. The letters were four inches tall so that even the visually impaired in the group could distinguish them. However, even those not able to 'see' the letters due to poor sight, or the lack of insight with dementia, were able to participate fully as many of the group called out the letter each time it was to be used. For each letter, the group were asked to give a word starting with that letter, and all the words should be associated with Valentine's Day and romantic love. As the men had declined to attend, all the participants were women, and they enthusiastically endeavoured to answer. To give an opportunity for slower response, the participants had to raise their hand when they had chosen a word. Answers such as 'virtue', 'virility' and 'amour' were chosen for the first two letters. 'Love' was lingered on with delight, as was the 'eagerness' of the loved one returning from the Second World War. 'N' proved to be the most hilarious, with one witty woman suggesting 'naughty but nice'. 'T' gave way to pathos as 'trauma' was suggested as the reaction that set in when their beloved men, including fathers and brothers, did not return home from war. Dora, with severe dementia, had been observed sitting in the activities group in the past, but not usually participating verbally in a way that could be understood. However, her response to the letter 'I' thrilled all of us in the group, when she suggested love and Valentine's Day as 'interesting'. The letters 'D' and 'Y' also proved to bring out deep memories, as all agreed with one woman's suggestion that 'D' represented the 'dreaming' in their present situations about their lost and dead love ones. 'Y' represented the 'yearning' to see loved ones whom they all painfully missed.

In addition to the letters written out boldly on card, all the participants were encouraged to draw an outline of a heart. Those who could not do so had it drawn for them and they were then able to colour it in with a felt tip pen. It was Dora again, who never talked, who drew a response from the care assistants later, when at supper and bed time she did not want to be parted from her drawing of the heart, and possibly what the heart represented for her.

On reflection, it is possible that the women were more liberated in their answers by participating in an all-women group that afternoon. Certainly, one of the men who had been asked to join in would not have enjoyed the light-hearted approach. Apart from his serious manner, his wife had recently died, so the reminiscence involved may well have been too much for him.

One other woman with dementia did not offer any suggestions of words, but was pleasantly animated, closely watching all that took place. Another woman with dementia who was single and had been a headmistress all her working life also joined in enthusiastically. She had been known to weep many times since being admitted to the care home, with the sheer frustration of not knowing where she was or why she was there. However, she was calm for a number of days after this activity, so it is certainly possible to access or engage with people suffering from dementia. For a lucid participant, such as Edwina with her 'naughty but nice', there was delight in what she saw as her risqué self!

On arrival at the nursing home the following day, the head of care and a number of care assistants were keen to relate how the residents involved in yesterday's activity kept talking about it through the evening. Apparently, two of the women with dementia were extremely animated, even though they cannot normally have a conversation unless their memory prompts are known. As already mentioned, Dora showed her coloured-in heart to anyone who would look and listen, telling people she had put it under her pillow. Dora had never married, and before the Second World War had been a model in Paris. All employees mentioned how thrilled they were with the outcome of the activity, particularly the continued animation of those who had participated so contentedly.

One feature of the work of the activities group was the production of a monthly newsletter consisting of an A4 sheet that contained news such as birthday celebrations and mention of residents who had died that month.

Space was given for a biography as narrated by residents themselves or sometimes by a relative if that resident was unable to communicate verbally. Profiles included that of Bob, who had cycled from Grimsby to Oxford during the depression of the 1930s, and gained employment as a butcher in the covered market in Oxford. He settled in Oxford, married and raised a family. Another profile told of a woman brought up in a village that is now a suburb of Oxford, and how she used to take tea out to the fields when the men were hay-making. Yet another woman described how she had worked at the car factory during the war, hand stitching the canvas to the framework of training planes. Some of the profiles described love of dancing, or sport such as cycling or soccer, so there was a bitter irony to the passive type of activity on offer by the therapist.

On discussing aspects of reminiscence evident in the newsletter profiles, I asked the leader if there was not a place for sharing this openly in the activities sessions as well as in printed form, as many of the residents would not be able to read the newsletter but could well respond to the narrative in a group session. She said that she was comfortable doing reminiscence therapy with the residents using a kit from a local museum of household utensils and artefacts from the Second World War, including a ration book, but she was unable to conduct sessions where the participants themselves brought to light things from their past. Asked if there was active involvement by residents in the production of the newsletter, she replied that it was quicker and more convenient for her son to do it on his word processor at home. It would have been fascinating to see what skills the various residents could have brought to the production of such a newsletter. In some ways, this highlights attitudes of infantilisation discussed earlier; in other ways, it shows aspects of the dangers of an institution thinking it can be all-providing in its care.

During a period when the occupational therapist was on holiday, I was invited by some of the care assistants to hold another activities session. It was thought that reminiscence through photographs might prove enjoyable and meaningful for the residents, so I brought in a selection of books borrowed from a public library. All these books contained reproductions of old photographs, taken at the turn of the century, of local towns and villages. One woman aged ninety-nine and her seventy-year-old daughter visiting for the afternoon were present, as were five other women, two of whom could not usually converse. Opportunity to attend had been given to a number of women and men who had declined. However, it was felt best to keep the numbers low so as those participating would be able to spend time over the books if they wanted to. One of the women present was not able to concentrate but all the others were actively involved with the photographs. Ten residents made up the session.

Although the photographs were of locations around the county, two residents who had moved to the home from other parts of the country participated and identified with what the photos represented, rather than the places themselves. For example, photos of horses and carriages, showing the uniform of the horsemen, as well as the fashions of the time, were recognised by all. What was most interesting was the quiet response from all the participants. They wanted to linger on each scene and take it in, quietly pointing out what they knew but with no endeavour to share their experiences with others in the group. As with other activities that I conducted on two other afternoons, it was the aftermath in the following days that showed what residents and employees thought. For example, one of the maintenance men brought in the original photo of his grandfather as reprinted in one of the books, driving a horse and carriage parked outside a mansion. He also brought in many photos of the MG sports car factory. Apparently, the male participant had told him about the photos he recognised, so the maintenance man then wanted to bring in his collection of photos, which he had taken during the last days of the factory's existence. A nurse who worked occasionally at the nursing home was also keen to share in the experiences engendered by the employee bringing in the photographs of the car factory. That the maintenance man and male visitors knew of my love of MG sports cars added to the richness and fun of the occasion.

Exclusion of Certain Residents from Activities

Significant by their absence at many of the activities held daily were people with dementia. There are many studies that show people with dementia can gain immense satisfaction and pleasure from structured activities. Kovach and Henschel (1996) looked at the planning of activities for patients with dementia among twenty-three women from two twelve-bed special care units in nursing homes. One of their key points noted was that the relief of boredom prevents behavioural problems.

Only occasionally did the activities leader encourage someone with dementia to participate in or sit with residents taking part in activities. Yet people like Sarah, diagnosed with dementia, were regularly encouraged to attend the bingo sessions conducted weekly by Moira and were seen to enjoy it. Apart from the community singing sessions, which were greatly enjoyed by many, no activities were planned to include people with dementia. When the activities organiser invited the residents beforehand to encourage them to attend the sessions, she rarely encouraged the residents with dementia. Bob, mentioned earlier lucidly describing himself as bored, was seldom given the opportunity to participate in activity sessions.

Cheryl, unable to communicate via speech, apart from shouting if distressed or bored, was often placed in an armchair alone in her room, with no company and little stimulus. At times, care assistants were concerned about this, stating that they wished there was something they could do for her. One early afternoon, they endeavoured to keep her seated in the conservatory, which had employees and residents walking by and often through it. However, with Cheryl's persistent shouting, other residents became cross and upset, one asking the question, 'Aren't there places for people like her?' Thinking the woman shouting could be pacified with some background music near her, I talked with the manager about the use of a cassette player or radio specifically in her room. The manager produced a radio that had been left by relatives of a resident who had died. Batteries were purchased for it that day and an electric connection later acquired. Classic FM was put on for a few hours for Cheryl and for some of the time she became much quieter. When it was played in the main lounge later for other residents to listen to, it was much appreciated by nearly all who listened. However, there were those who did not enjoy it and these may well have been people who did not listen to classical music in the course of their lifetime; when the local radio station was put on, they enjoyed it more. The overall effect of the music being played that afternoon, however, was of a more peaceful atmosphere. One care assistant brought 'Jim Reeves' cassette tapes to play on the radio cassette after the activities were over in the hour before tea was served.

Within a few weeks, the manager had confiscated the radio, saying that the care assistants constantly played a pop station. She would not be persuaded that this was not the case, the radio station being changed only occasionally. The environment consequently returned to one without music and the ever-present noise of a television. So, in the course of the study, no specific activity was seen to be geared towards the residents with dementia, even though music, in particular, is seen to be therapeutic in residential settings. Except for the irregular sessions of community singing, when people with dementia felt able and encouraged to join in, little formal activity was arranged for them.

Activities and Residents' Responses

During some celebrations of birthdays, sherry was offered and music provided, as noted during one much-enjoyed afternoon in early spring-time consisting of 'songs that won the war'. Many residents danced, and three of the four who had been in institutions for most of their adult lives took part with gusto. All of them commented on the provision of weekly dances in the psychiatric hospitals as a much-loved activity. One resident, who had a career as a psychiatric nurse, was adept at involving less able and shy residents in the dancing. It was one of the liveliest activity sessions observed, and produced much enthusiasm from both residents and care assistants, with the residents appearing content as well as animated by their experience.

In the days prior to Easter, the manager bought Easter eggs for all the residents, to be given out on Easter Sunday. By lunch time, none of the residents had received them, so I enquired of the staff as to when the eggs were going to be given to the residents. Management stated that they were to be given with afternoon tea at 3 p.m. It seemed that there was a certain amount of control taking place with the handing out of these eggs; part of the fun of Easter eggs is to eat them and enjoy them as soon as possible. One of the care assistants said 'they are not allowed to have them yet'.

During spring-time, talk was of the coming Easter and how in the activities groups in previous years they had made Easter bonnets and planted seeds to grow in pots. However, no similar activity had been arranged for this year, which the residents found disheartening. In early summer, expectations were of making bunting for the summer fete, but on the afternoon when they should have begun, the activities session was cancelled as the activities leader was away. On another afternoon, also allocated for the making of the bunting for the fete, the person who was to show how it was done did not arrive, and as the leader did not have anything else arranged, the activities session was cancelled. The manager did not always know about such cancellations but, in time, was informed by residents as well as care assistants, who all showed concern at the increased level of boredom. Some activities sessions, such as hand exercises, were over within half an hour, resulting in residents complaining that they would have liked a longer session. The previous activities sessions would last between two and two-and-a-half hours. One woman commented that she was 'really fed up with the activities therapist, as there is always too much chat'. Others despairingly called the talks 'homely'. Wynona, who said she wished that their 'grey matter was stretched more', when asking the occupational therapist what activities would be held that afternoon was told it would be a 'talk-about'. Wynona turned and raised her eyebrows with a look of desperation on her face. Most of the women had been active all their lives, either in part-time work outside their homes or as full-time housewives and mothers. They expressed the wish for more 'doing' rather than sitting inactively for long hours. Two of the women in wheelchairs, who had paralysis of an arm and leg after suffering a stroke, wished to be more active, one being given the paper napkins to fold for meal times and the other trying to keep 'sane' by attempting word games from the Sunday newspapers. Only three residents were seen at any time reading a book, while many of the women were not interested in the kind of television programmes on all day and would purposefully avoid the areas where the television sets were on.

On afternoons during good weather, those who were independently mobile were encouraged to walk in the garden down to the riverside, where many river craft could be seen. Some of the care assistants made time to take the less able person on a walk or in a wheelchair into the garden and down to the river. One relative, a husband of a resident, regularly took his wife into the garden in a wheelchair so they could sit there together. However, one problem in using the garden via the conservatory exit was its limitation to wheelchair users or people using walking frames or walking sticks. As mentioned earlier, there was a raised lip where the entrance joined the garden steps, which also restricted movement for people not totally mobile. Staff as well as residents mentioned this to the manager and Head Office personnel many times during the course of the study, specifically requesting the building of a ramp from the entrance to the garden. This was not followed up by the manager, even though employees and residents made repeated requests for it to be attended to. The portion of garden which led out from the conservatory was private in that it could not be viewed from the main road, and was also secure in that staff could see who was in the garden at any time. Three of the male residents had spent much time in their own gardens at home, one man, John, relating how he spent more time in his greenhouse than in his actual home. He had difficulty accessing the home's garden as he used a walking frame. He was also a cigarette smoker and said that he would have liked the opportunity to smoke in the garden when the weather was good. The gardens were well maintained and, in places, the lawn looked manicured. It was always an aspect of the nursing home favourably commented on by relatives as it leads down to the banks of a main river.

Informal Activities and Their Stimuli

Sybil, a resident, had a career as an artist, carrying on well beyond retirement age. Her nephew visited often and each time he had a selection of postcards that were sent to Sybil from all over the world during her lifetime. She had progressive dementia until she died, but he would place the picture or design in front of her asking her if she knew it. Then he would read the message written by a friend and ask her if she remembered who the friend was and where they were from. He was often able to stimulate a response from her in this way and said that he felt satisfied at being able to do it for her. He brought in photographs of a recent holiday he had in Goa, describing every scene to her and encouraging a response. Each time he visited and shared with her in this way, he was convinced that she responded to him and the objects he brought with him. I told him about the time I had taken her out in the garden in a wheelchair and, when near the riverside, she recognised and named the chimney stacks at the power station across the river, without being prompted, showing that she would readily respond to stimuli.

Some, like the nephew just mentioned, were better able to relate to their relatives than others. One young man used to visit his aunt, to whom he had been very close over the years, and managed to get her to speak to his mother, her sister, on his mobile phone. Another resident, Wynona, enjoyed being prompted about her past. She preferred to do this in the privacy of her own room, where ornaments of a dog and a horse as well as drawings and photographs of them testified to her love of animals. She stressed what a private person she was, preferring her own company or that of her well-loved dogs of many years. The china dog was a retriever, reminiscent of her last dog, which had to be put down by the vet as she was being admitted to the home. She discussed her love of animals and how her son was trying to get a variety of photos together to form a collage of animals for her room. She used to walk her dogs at 4.30 a.m. if she woke early in the summer, and could remember walking the dogs in the Peak District as a child. During the moments talking about her animals, she also spoke of riding her own thoroughbred horse as a child and teenager. This led on to describing her father as a 'businessman but a tap dancer and comedian in his spare time'. One aunt was particularly musical, so the family shared much music together. Wynona could remember vividly the photographs of her grandmother dressed in a crinoline skirt, saying that she still had the photographs packed away in her room.

Much of the stimulus occurs on a one-to-one basis between resident and care assistant or other staff members. Emilia, who had once said to me, 'Oh I am so lonely', needed company so I sat with her as often as possible, talking mainly about her days in service in a large manor house. When in her late teens, she had to leave her home in the north of England and travel to Oxfordshire looking for work, as there were five children in the family, as well as an aunt living with them. We discussed what the manor was presently used for, and she was pleased when responding to the memory prompts, gleaned from conversations with her daughter and granddaughter. Each time, she would reply, 'Oh how lovely' and 'Isn't it nice to share these things'. One of the care assistants did not know these biographical details, but was keen thereafter to use the biography as conversation prompts. If there is limited conversation, as in this case due to dementia, then biographical knowledge of the person is important in being able to preserve memory recall, to engage in conversation and to motivate the person. Repeated reminders as to time and place are often necessary. Earlier in our conversation, Emilia had said she thought it was warm for February, until being reminded that it was June and therefore midsummer.

Conversely, Cheryl, the woman who shouted for prolonged periods of time, regularly sat alone in her room, which had bare walls and few ornaments or mementoes present. There was little or no stimulus until a care assistant or her husband, a local shopkeeper in the market town, entered the room. There was rarely music on in her room or in the conservatory where she sat, after the manager confiscated the radio.

On seeing the nursing home cat cleaning itself in the sun one morning, Rose and Rowena began to talk about pets. The cat itself was brought in with a woman who, on admission, did not want to be parted from it. Rose had been really upset when her cat was put down when ill with an infection. She still felt a sense of loss two years later. Arthur, severely impaired with dementia, often expressed grief at the death of his pet dog, talking about it more often than his wife. Both Rose and Rowena talked often about the need for people to express their depression and boredom at living an institutional life.

Both women wanted reassurance, at various times, that the sale of their houses and furniture had taken place and that the transactions had been dealt with by relatives. One was particularly upset when her furniture was sold. As mentioned earlier, on the day of the furniture sale she had been jokingly asked the question, 'Have you got your happy head on today then Rose, or your sad one?' by a member of the kitchen staff. The employee, who was not aware of what was happening in Rose's private life, was seen to encourage similarly depressed residents to see the 'bright side'. These are painful stimuli for people desperately trying to come to terms with significant losses of spouse, home, possessions and pets.

The regular complaint from Edwina, Wynona and others that they felt the activity sessions to be lacking in stimulus and quality concurs with Kayser-Jones' conclusion that 'if social activities are of poor quality, not only are they boring, but also demeaning' (1981: 30). The effects of boredom are noticeable; residents become increasingly listless and find excuses not to attend sessions that they felt from experience would not be stimulating. In a 1992 Counsel and Care study, tellingly entitled 'Not Only Bingo', respondents rated highly the opportunity to take part in activities (Counsel and Care 1992: 7). As well as people living in residential homes, older people living in their own homes were included in the survey. What they feared most was the monotony, even ennui. Many different activities are encountered in residential homes, for example arts and crafts, bridge parties, pottery, photography and frame-making (1992: 14). An observation made to me by one staff member was that there should be anticipation of and allowance for requests to install home computers belonging to future residents, who may well be computer literate.

Many of the women interviewed would have benefited from opportunities to assist in tasks in running the home. When Glenys was first admitted, she constantly wished to help and could have easily managed light dusting, or washing up afternoon tea cups, with little supervision. One of the care assistants would give Amy the opportunity to dry dishes after tea time. She looked so pleased to be doing it and managed it well. The woman who sat and 'shadow dusted' a table may well have enjoyed being given a duster to use. This kind of stimulation is so familiar to women who have spent a lifetime as homemakers, but can be lost in an institution that can so easily become all-providing. The manager suggested to the activities leader that she encourage Sarah to wash up all the cups, and although this was not taken up by the activities leader, the manager did not pursue it, saying that she was unable to 'motivate' her. When women such as those mentioned here spoke of boredom, they also spoke of wishing that the staff had more time to sit and talk with them. It is the special relationship and vicarious living that meet the individual's needs where possible and when workload permits. The desire for company and for a 'listening ear' was a significant factor in this researcher becoming accepted quickly by the residents.

Along with written guidelines, as mentioned, there are known practices incorporated into the life of the care home and activities sessions that alleviate boredom and provide stimulation for the residents. For instance, as described earlier, the photos of places at the turn of the century were favourably received and located in terms of reminiscence for the participants. The activities therapist, on just one occasion, was observed conducting a reminiscence session using artefacts rented from a local museum as a pack for such groups. The residents reminisce at times among themselves, but say they prefer to nostalgically remember with staff and visitors, including the researcher, as they were passing on their knowledge of life itself. Consequently, the years of the war, as well as postwar issues such as rationing, featured greatly in their accounts. However, in a task-oriented environment such as the care home, with an emphasis on getting the job in hand done, the time for reminiscence, guided by employees, takes a low priority. In reality, though, taking part in reminiscence sessions enables staff to become more aware of individual personalities, leading to a more personal communication and understanding. This is the kind of communication and understanding that residents expressed a yearning for, and probably relieves the kind of boredom they experienced and talked about. Often they want empathy for events they have lived through, sometimes the world-changing events of world wars.

The reality of life is that reminiscence is not always possible, as the younger generation has its own life events and cultural markers. But it must be part of the responsibility of people who lead activities sessions to ensure that stimuli occur, and the despair of boredom is avoided. That this is also the responsibility of management and staff is self-evident. The most elderly residents were over ninety years old, so an acknowledged understanding of the events affecting their lives would not have gone amiss. These events set the social and cultural context in which their values were formed and, while not all are world events, they pertain to a life lived individually and in their own communities and neighbourhoods.

The Ministry of Religion

Any discussion or evidence of religion and spirituality inside the home was notable by its absence; it was almost a taboo subject. Religion was an off-limits subject of conversation among residents, between staff and residents, and certainly between residents and their relatives. This could well be attributed to its association with death, which was rarely discussed. There were at least ten women residents who had been regular Anglican Church members, but these women did not get visits from an Anglican minister of religion. They had all moved to the home away from their home parishes. Halfway through the study, an Anglican minister began to visit regularly when a retired schoolteacher was admitted, though he only visited her. A Catholic nun visited two men and one woman weekly, and was chauffeured each time by a male colleague who would sit in the dining area and wait for her to finish. Upon asking him what he did, he explained that he was a priest, but showed no inclination to visit with residents in the time he spent in the home, nor did the nun visit residents other than those from her own 'flock'.

When asking the Anglican minister why he visited Joyce and no one else, he replied that he did not know the other Anglican residents. As residents such as Wynona had told me of her loyalty and love for the church, and residents such as Sybil had raised money for church funds during her life, it seemed that the church was not there to cheer and encourage them in what was a difficult time in their lives. There were also other residents who had tenuous links with the church throughout their lives but whose beliefs were aligned with the church's teachings. They would have benefited from stronger contact with a minister of religion and the church. In this nursing home, the evident lack of addressing issues such as religion, death and dying could well have been due to the lack of participation by a minister or parish church members rather than the unwillingness of the staff themselves. On the rare occasions when such matters were discussed, staff, mainly nurses, expressed their felt inadequacy at dealing with them. This concurs with Butler (1996), who when looking at worship in residential care found that there was lack of opportunity among residents to observe their beliefs, resulting in significant loss of identity and community.

One activity that took place monthly was the visit to the nursing home on a Saturday afternoon by a group of evangelical Christians. Christianity was the only religion represented by residents in the home. Residents who showed an interest in religion and organised activities attended the programme offered by this evangelical group, who stressed that they did not represent any particular church or denomination. The group began to visit in this capacity after the mother of one of the group members was cared for in the home until her death. On arrival in one of the lounges, the group members would encourage people seated there to turn their chairs a certain way towards where the group were standing. Sometimes the care assistants facilitated this beforehand and arranged some of the chairs. This also gave residents the opportunity to move out of the area if they did not want to take part in the service. Two women, two men and a dog formed the group, who provided a form of worship in each of the three lounges. One of the men played the guitar and sang along with the women. Song sheets were handed out for residents to participate in the singing, but often impromptu choruses and prayer songs were sung which many of the residents did not appear to know. What follows here is a description of one afternoon of worship observed during the year.

Wynona, who was in her usual corner of the lounge, had been a lifelong member of the Church of England and a regular churchgoer. Ula sat nearby in a wheelchair. She was a great singer at any time, bursting forth into song during the day, but we were not aware of any church interests as she had lost the ability to communicate verbally due to dementia. Rowena and Cecil sat next to Florence, Joan and Maisie. There was a semi-circle of four women, seated, and Emilia as usual seated alone at a table. She was excited about what was taking place, saying afterwards how the constant monotony of her life in the home was relieved. Emma sat at a distant dining table, appearing not to join in, as she often stressed that she only mixed with people she chose. In another area of the lounge sat a half circle of women, namely Molly, Mary and Sybil, all suffering from various stages of dementia. Two of these women had been churchgoers prior to admission to the home. The singers then turned two chairs normally facing the television to face towards where they were to conduct the service. Women residents were seated in them when they did this. Edwina was in her usual spot by the side of the television.

Song sheets in large print were handed out and at first glance many songs appeared unknown. However, on the chorus of the first one, many residents joined in and afterwards said that it was a chorus they had learnt while living in the home. Wynona did not sing but sat contentedly, whereas Cecil voiced his opinion that he was not really interested. It transpired later that he did not know that he had a choice about whether or not to be present.

During the service, which consisted of singing and prayer, a scripture reading was given, describing Jesus Christ healing women with a haemorrhage. This is a well-known miracle in Christian circles, and one of the women leading the service addressed the group of residents gathered, saying, 'He wants people that are healthy and well, not sick. Anyone who wants to be well should ask God'. The other woman member of the group testified to God healing her of arthritis, emphasising that she had been really sick. One woman resident called out, 'Well he hasn't healed my arthritis'. This comment was not addressed by any member of the group, who then rounded off the half-hour service by praying for everyone to be healed. The prayer included the phrase that God would only heal people if they first confessed their sins to Him. During the prayer time, the residents were asked if any of them wanted a group member to pray with them, but no requests were made. The woman who read the Bible did so with an American accent, but in conversation she reverted to her English accent. When singing, one of the men also sang with an American accent, common in evangelical circles, but spoke with an English accent in conversation. This was wryly remarked on by Wynona, who had been a member of the Anglican Church all her life.

The visiting group then moved to another lounge with one resident, Sarah, following. This lounge, like all lounges in the home, had some immobile residents sitting there, or people who could not move with ease. They were a captive audience as no opportunity had been given for them to leave the lounge before the service started. One of the women was to read the Bible, but the other said there was not enough time left as tea would be served at 5 p.m. (it was already 4.50 when the service started). Instead, she quoted a verse from the Bible, saying 'I am the way, the truth and the life', and then told the group of residents that if they had not already asked the Lord into their lives, they should do so. She laid emphasis on 'accepting the Lord before it is too late'. Jennifer, a care assistant, was sitting with Ethel whose head was on the table. Suddenly, Ethel looked up and in a loud voice said, 'Well then are all the people well satisfied?' Ethel's comment and observation was interesting, as it was one of the few times she was heard to speak and appeared to show an understanding of what was taking place. The group then collected the song sheets, said farewell and left. Upon observing the group conducting services on other occasions, the style and content followed the same evangelical format, with staff describing the group as 'clap happys' in a disparaging manner. However, the deputy head of care informed me of an occasion that gave rise to concern for all the staff present. Care assistants and nurses were troubled at the group members praying with some residents and 'laying hands' on some people's heads. No agreement from the individual residents concerned had been asked for or given, and the greatest problem surrounded a resident who had been confined to a psychiatric hospital for many years prior to admission to the nursing home. It took place near the end of a service in the lounge when one of the evangelicals had laid hands on Cora's head and prayed over her, possibly 'in tongues', without Cora's request or agreement. Cora was observed by care staff to enter 'one of her staring, zombie type phases'. These phases rarely occurred, but when one did, she would need much reassurance from the care assistants and nurses during the episode and afterwards. It was also reported that a group member had laid hands on Cecil's head, who afterwards asked what he had done to deserve it. The deputy head of care was so incensed by the incidents that she wrote a letter of complaint to management notifying them, stating what she felt to be an invasion of privacy and lack of choice. The manager then contacted the group and expressed her concern that a 'vulnerable group of people' had been taken advantage of. They were still able to visit the home and conduct services, although staff members were more likely to sit and observe the service than before. That there is a place for sensitive ministry is not disputed. What was of concern here was the invasion of a person's private space, especially when she/he was not able to protest.

One of the problems in attending to the spiritual needs of people is that these needs are seen to be located within the domain of a minister of religion. The care assistants and the nurses said they benefited personally from the visit by a priest or minister of religion to a dying resident. Staff felt that it was an essential part of the care of the dying person, but that they did not feel equipped to do this themselves. That such a ministerial visit did not always happen indicated a lack of a holistic view in caring for the person. Staff members need to respect all aspects of life other than the social, physical and psychological, so that once identified, spiritual needs can be appropriately included and addressed. This is especially so at the time a dying person is being cared for, when it is more than possible to see a spiritual dimension in work carried out by a care assistant or nurse. In this home, awareness of the needs of the relative was seen during these times, with a general harmony evident between relatives and staff members. Attention to the detail of care seemed somehow sharper, more sensitive and involved a higher level of care than normal. This detailed care of the resident extended to attendance at the funeral by the main carer, nurse or care assistant as their way of showing love and respect. The care for the resident shown had more often than not been reciprocated by the resident in a relationship lasting for months, if not years. Loving relationships are often established. It is important to note here that in the silence surrounding death, the demise of a resident was rarely discussed in the presence of other residents, who would only learn of the death in a circuitous way. In the same way that children are protected from the reality of the death of a loved one, here we can see again the infantilisation of the older person as an institutionalised resident.

Church members and clergy may find illnesses such as dementia difficult to face, certainly something noted when talking with the priest who would sit alone and wait for the nun. Some church members excuse themselves from visiting nursing homes, due to the fear of ageing or a wish to avoid such issues. Dementia is a challenge to any church congregation, as it is to society at large, but it would seem that Christian communities in response to their members in care homes could improve their ministry to people with dementia as well as to staff. As with reminiscence therapy, the spiritual well-being of people with dementia could be enhanced from the prompting of memory of faith, best done through music and appropriate readings.

Some residents who were not able to make conversation were well able to join in traditional prayers such as the Lord's Prayer. When gospel songs or hymns were sung, it was noted that people with dementia who did not speak joined in by humming along with the singing. There is evidence here of the remembrance of learned worship. Therefore, a church member or minister liaising with the residents and staff and occasionally taking a resident to church could have been a beneficial initiative. If ministers of religion had visited, they may have found that they strengthened what the staff endeavoured to do for the residents, especially during the time of dying. The kind of pastoral care offered by ministers of religion, particularly to support the care of the dying, could also be a vital support for staff members who face the issues of death among themselves. The tradition of care assistants and other staff members attending funerals shows their acknowledgement of the spiritual dimensions to their work. They, like the residents, need opportunities to express this. To be able to openly discuss the death or dying of a resident would lead to a more enriching approach to living and ultimately dying in the twenty-first century.

Chapter 5
ORDERING DISORDER

❧

Do not go gentle into that good night, Old age should burn and rave at close of
day; Rage, rage against the dying of the light.
—Dylan Thomas, 'Do Not Go Gentle Into That Good Night'

Having observed the daily routine of a year in the life of the care home and
discussed these research findings here the focus will be on concerns arising within the routine of care work. These concerns include the impact of
living as a group on individual privacy, the impact of inactivity on morale,
the loneliness of loss, and the overall quality of life for both resident and
employee.

Firstly, however, two aspects of the study should be mentioned that did
not feature in the ethnography but are worthy of further research. These two
areas were conspicuous by their absence in my field notes, namely death and
finances. Thirteen residents died during the course of the study, sometimes
while I was present, and during these sad times much care was shown to the
dying person, as well as to the relatives, by care assistants and other staff.
Within the daily routine, however, death was not a topic often addressed by
care assistants or other staff in conversation or workplace discussion, formal
or informal. Even at the time of a resident's death, it was rarely heard being
discussed. It could be that because this study was addressing issues to do
with life as lived in the nursing home, death would not feature prominently,
even when expected. However, it is also part of the reserve that surrounds
death within the society in which we live, with remnants of the Victorian
approach whereby death is to be faced with stoicism and to be hidden from
view. Health care professionals both here and in other care settings say they
find it difficult to discuss issues of death and bereavement, though care
assistants did say that if they told residents of a fellow resident's death, they
could at least all be part of the period of grieving within the home. One clear
observation regarding death was that the staff, care assistants, hairdresser and

manager were especially keen to attend funerals of residents whom they had cared for and got to know over the years. There was always great disappointment if staff were unable to attend a funeral service; they said they felt it was part of their final care and respect for the resident.

There is also a definite silence within my data concerning finances and money. On a number of occasions, questions directed to the administrator were answered with a rather swift request to return on another occasion. Early on in the study, one woman with dementia, sitting dozing in the open lounge, suddenly awoke to ask, 'Where's my pension?' No one could give her an answer, and in discussion with care assistants it became obvious that residents did not have cash on them, some saying that none of their pension seemed to be allocated back to them personally. This could not be ascertained or clarified, no matter how often the accountant was asked about it. All that was given in answer was that the resident's needs were completely cared for on admission to the home and that some of their individual pensions were used towards chiropody and needs such as new clothes or shoes. It was also difficult to gain an understanding of the overall financial aspect of this privately run nursing home. That some of the residents were funded by social services seemed to make it even more difficult to gain information on the finances. Hence the silences within the data.

The main issue in this concluding chapter represents the achievement of order in any given day, which was predominantly the accomplishment of care assistants and nurses working on the morning shift. Other shifts had their routines in the afternoons, evenings and night times but it was primarily the morning shift where the attainment of order was perceived to be the goal, along with an almost corporate sigh of relief when all residents were seen to be seated in their comfortable chairs relaxing and anticipating lunch. For most staff, that order did not come at the expense of attention to the residents, but was incorporated into every last detail of care, whether the workload was 'heavy' or not. It exemplifies routine for both the resident and the employee. This observation of the daily routine shows that it can actually be life-enhancing to the resident, who is dependent upon someone carrying out that routine for them, the attendance to activities of daily living. It also represents the way of life of the home itself and the palpable feeling of success when that 'order' was achieved. When all the activities of daily living, such as hairdresser appointments, take place in the home, there is a lingering sense of Goffman's 'total institution', even though his bleak portrayal of daily life in asylums may well be over. Mali (2008) also mentions this trend for de-institutionalisation of similar care homes for older people in Slovenia.

Some researchers have found that the rules in place in nursing homes are designed with staff in mind, and all residents are to be treated the same in order to make tasks simpler for the staff. Lidz, Fischer and Arnold (1992:

105) established that all patients were treated more or less as 'identical problems to be managed'. However, in the present study, such a rigid interpretation of rules on the part of the workforce was not found. What was observed though, especially for people with dementia, was a consistent routine that regularly structured the day for the person, especially if they had lost the cognitive capacity to do so themselves. Also, for many residents, it would seem that the very routine, particularly that of the busy morning schedule, led to a calm order rather than regimentation. Within the achieved order that regularly took place in the private space of the bedrooms, attributes were seen contributing to a quality of life for the resident, such as being seated in the lounge next to someone known or liked rather than sitting alone in their room. For example, Edwina, residing on what she called the 'chaotic' wing, frequently missed her weekly bath if the shift was particularly hectic due to shortage of staff, which happened often. She was quick to state how she felt about this, as it caused her much distress. Her use of the word 'chaotic' and other cryptic remarks showed that she was aware of what produced calm and order for residents during any morning routine. When the wing was calm following one particular morning routine during which she was bathed, her satisfaction was evident to all coming in contact with her. Edwina herself said, 'What is needed is more of a routine', pointing out that she had always had her own routine when living at home. She said that she appreciated it when care assistants from other wings helped, and felt that this showed the staff's flexibility and that they were not 'too rigid'. She appreciated having the opportunity to discuss when and how she wanted things done to her and for her, and above all what she could do herself. Care assistants working in a systematic way through their busy morning schedule on other wings rarely encountered the kind of disorder or 'chaos' seen on the wing where Edwina lived, and rightly felt that on the two wings where staff followed a routine, there was a certain level of flexibility, even in light of staff shortages.

Within this routine, the 'ordering' of a resident takes place but was seen by most residents as being necessary. Residents who could communicate often reiterated that they could not perform the tasks of daily living such as washing and dressing by themselves, so were glad of the assistance and attention consistently given. The personal chaos and disorder associated with physical illness as well as dementia can be seen to subside in the midst of the routine, including that of the physical environment, such as the making of the bed and the tidying of the room. However, what can enhance the routine is the way in which the tasks are carried out by the care assistant. If the task of washing someone or helping a resident onto a commode, for example, is performed in a caring and thoughtful way, and not just with the end product in mind, as in a task-oriented approach, then the routine itself becomes a positive aspect of life within the nursing home, improving individual quality of life. But what does doing a job in this way entail on the part of the care assistant? Attention to detail for the person being washed or sat on a commode would include such action as a curtain being drawn around the resident if the room is shared, and ensuring the room door is properly closed. Attention to personal matters, such as the flannel being used on the person's face before their bottom and covering up the body while washing other parts of it, demonstrates thoughtfulness to the tasks being performed by the care assistant. Lee-Treweek's (1997) pertinent observation that it is in the private space of a resident's bedroom that the processing of a clean orderly quiet resident takes place can also be seen in a positive rather than solely a negative sense. If, for example, the order arising from the routine care undertaken by the care assistant enables a person with dementia to feel safe and free from anxiety and harm, then the research findings suggest that the 'end result' could well include the presence of quality of life. Sitting in a comfortable chair in good company, or waiting expectantly for a musical activity to begin, could be seen as significant attributes that contribute to quality of life in a way that the disordered, chaotic work style does not. It was the disorder of a person's life at home, such as Doreen's, mentioned earlier in a case study, that led to her admission to the nursing home. In particular, Doreen's cousin expressed that he could not bear the thought of her living in the house with cat faeces and human faeces smeared around it, so admission to the nursing home was, on balance, the most caring thing to do for her. It seems then that the creating of order out of disorder through routine can be a positive aspect within the definition of home as used in the term 'care or nursing home'. It becomes a negative characteristic when the extreme order of task-orientation that so often occurs at meal times takes priority over individual need, such as the nurse giving medication to residents without a word of greeting or comment. This was a task that had to be completed, ticked off on the 'to-do-list', and absence of the human touch was very noticeable. The fact that this took place at the beginning of the day, before breakfast, further demonstrated the absence of communication; even the normal 'good morning' was not spoken.

Although for the care assistant there is little respite from the daily round of routine tasks, it is the human interaction that brings light relief, as compared, say, to the repetitive tasks of a factory production line. These routine tasks described in Chapter 2 as performed by the care assistant are often intimate ones, such as bathing a person or taking someone to the toilet, and even wiping a person's bottom. It is the human contact, not only the tactile nature of touch but especially conversation, that ensures the quality of life associated with caring work is preserved within the much-needed procedures and health care practice. It is also in the eye for detail, for example when taking Thelma in her wheelchair to the toilet, noticing that the seat is wet with urine from a male resident who had used it before her. Thelma felt that she mattered if the seat was wiped first, however busy the care assistant was. Conversely, she felt indignant if this was not undertaken, especially if the procedure was performed so hurriedly that the wet seat was not noticed until she sat on it. For many of the routine duties, such as putting someone to bed or feeding someone, the process can become much more than a job to be completed if performed with a word, a smile or a touch. Add to that the humour and banter between resident and staff that is often apparent, and one can see the constant attempts at humanising the encounters within the routine. For most of the care assistants and staff, this was the case.

Even in the midst of a busy routine, the staff found time to keep the human aspect integral to their work. Lidz, Fischer and Arnold's (1992) American study found that the identical treatment of patients by staff was not only the rule but had become a 'fundamentally normative experience among line staff' (1992: 105). Although this was not the norm in the care home here, there were areas where it was noticed, as shown by the request from Marge, Edwina and Rowena to be allowed a cup of tea at times other than those allocated. There were also some residents who wished to get up at a different time in the morning, and occasionally this was respected. I observed this one morning when working with Chris, one of the care assistants. She showed flexibility in offering to return to attend to Benjamin later, as he wanted to stay in bed longer. The routine of having only one bath a week was also commented upon by women residents, who said they would like them more frequently. However, the residents mentioning this, such as Edwina or Wynona, would always excuse the staff, saying they knew how busy care assistants and nurses were most mornings, and that more baths would be difficult to fit into their schedule. But their understanding and sympathy for the workload of the care assistant did not stop them voicing their real desire for more than the regulated bath times, as well as an expression of individuality.

Linked in with the concept of routine is the evidence of a task-centred approach in care homes. If, as happens with some care assistants, the aim is to get the job done as quickly as possible, then task-centredness becomes the norm. Add to this the busy extra schedule that staff shortage inflicts, and one can see that the imperative is to complete all the tasks, especially before the mid-morning coffee time. Other evidence of a task-centred approach concerned dressing residents in clothes returned from the laundry, with some residents not being able to protest at what they were being dressed in. Surprised to see Elizabeth wearing a dress much too large for her one morning, I checked the label. The dress belonged to another woman of the same name, who was tall and broad in stature compared to Elizabeth. Because of the task-centred approach, the fit of the dress was not observed by the care assistant who had dressed Elizabeth that day. Task-centredness entails simply getting the job done, whereas if the care assistant had observed the surname on the label as well as the way the dress hung on Elizabeth, she would have realised that the dress belonged to another resident. Elizabeth, suffering with dementia, was not able to communicate easily, but it is possible that this kind of care led in some way to more loss of self-identity for her. It is likely that she knew from the way the dress hung, as well as the material and style of the dress, that it did not belong to her even if she was not able to express it in ways that could be understood.

Another area in which routine is paramount is the serving of meals. It is here that one notices how important it is to residents for meals to be served on time and to be served hot. If there is a shortage of staff in the kitchen, resulting in delay, there is much disquiet and discontent among the residents, especially if the manager had taken on the job of cook for the day. Able-bodied residents were encouraged by the staff to be seated at their tables for lunch some ten minutes before it is served, while less able-bodied people are guided and brought to their seats. If there was a delay in serving lunch, then agitation was noticeable. As mentioned in Chapter 4, music is a great soother at meal times, but this was not introduced until the study had ended. As with other routines in the nursing home, meal times can all too easily become task-oriented, with the goal of finishing being uppermost in the minds of staff. This can result in some residents not completing their meals in the time given, and having their unfinished meal taken away from them. When people needed to be fed by a staff member, it was noted that some care assistants seemed more concerned with the task of emptying the dish or plate rather than the individual eating characteristics of the resident concerned. This is where Kayser-Jones' (1996: 31) observation that all nursing assistants should be trained in meal-giving is of such importance, assisting in the creation of a pleasant social event.

Until this happens, trays with unfinished food will continue to be taken away from people who are still hungry but unable to feed themselves or voice that they have not finished. If the care assistants in the dining area serving two wings were freed up from washing dishes and emptying the dish steriliser, and with the kind of provision for individual meal time care that Kayser-Jones mentions, then one may begin to see meal times becoming more of a social event. While meal times remain task-focused, they will not be as pleasurable as they could be.

What was evident in the task-centred approach to meal times was the urgency of getting crockery washed and ready for a subsequent course, such as dessert or coffee. This sense of haste brought about by a shortage of crockery, and often by the extra strain of staff shortage, led to a consistently high level of noise in the dining area of one particular wing. That this was also the wing that lacked a consistent morning routine was accentuated by the fact that the nurse-in-charge was discontent, constantly letting other staff members know that she did not like working there or in any area to do with care of older people. When she resigned and was not replaced, the shortage of staff and the mayhem of meal times continued, particularly at lunch times. In the study of 100 local authority old people's homes, Peace, Kellaher and Willcocks (1982) said that in all the homes surveyed, meals were over in less than half an hour, except for the most incapacitated residents. More than three decades later, as shown here, the rush at meal times persists and the need for a meal-friendly environment is seen to be imperative, as reviewed by Abbott et al. (2013).

Keeping this idea of routine, order and disorder in the nursing home within the concept of quality of life, I now look at some of the characteristics of the 'total institution'. The nursing home does not fit the original total institution model, but it is worth noting some characteristics that fall into the model, or not as the case may be. In fact, this chapter highlights that within a care home, and by nature of its make-up, an institution can be found to have the desired ideals that make it a 'home from home' for residents and less of a 'total institution'.

Living as a Group versus Individual Privacy

One of the characteristics of total institution is all aspects of life being carried out in one place, whereas in modern society individuals usually sleep, play and work in different places. Evidence of this in the care home is found in the example of the twice-monthly chiropodist visits. Having the chiropodist visit the home means the residents miss an opportunity for a rare trip outside the home. Trips to a local hairdresser are also never made, as all hairdressing for men and women is done by the female hairdresser employed in the home. Equally, no resident during the whole course of the study was taken on a trip to church or to a pub. More importantly, what becomes clear here is that the activities of daily living are not only carried out under one roof but are performed in the presence of so many people. Often these activities can be undertaken without attention to detail. As was observed on one occasion, for example, a nurse uncovered Albert's penis in the lounge to check on his catheter. One again notes here the negative impact of a task-centred environment, prioritising getting the job done even to the detriment of personal privacy. Total institution does not allow for time or leeway between jobs. It is this inherent characteristic that led the nurse to check Albert's penis in public instead of taking him somewhere private. This is where the tension between maintaining a necessary routine and the heavily regimented confines of a time scale is seen. Occasionally, observation was made of both male and female residents' underwear and tights being pulled up in public, in the open lounge areas for example, the practice of which is criticised in guidelines for promoting standards in residential and nursing homes (Residential Forum 1996; Mulley et al. 2015). My findings show that it is the loss of privacy, dignity and self-esteem that people fear most when moving into a home. The exposure of their personal habits to other residents and their awareness of other residents' habits is dreaded.

Examples of what people fear most include sharing a table with a poor eater at meal times, and particularly the sharing of a bedroom. As discussed earlier concerning use of a toilet, residents with single bedrooms and en-suite facilities managed to keep these personal habits, which they fear being exposed, within the bounds of privacy. In shared bedrooms, curtains may manage to give some privacy, but they do not shut out bodily noises and odours. However, in the example above involving Albert, he would have had to be taken from the lounge to his own room to be afforded the kind of privacy needed to look at his catheter, so even though the institution itself has procedures in place for providing privacy, it is the nurse or staff member's own interpretation of what is acceptable within the institution that takes precedence. Guidelines for an individual's privacy stress that older people as well as their older relatives are not always assertive in their hoped-for endeavour for dignity and privacy.

Albert was often assertive in shouting aloud when he wanted attention, for example changing the television channel, but even in the presence of a nurse who represented a certain amount of authority, he was not at all understanding about any rights or preferences his fellow residents may also wish to assert. The care assistants all stated at the end of this study the real need for adequate training, including attention to dignity and the guarding of the resident's privacy. It is evident within the media stories in the UK that nurses' attention or lack of attention to patients' dignity and privacy should be a priority for both institutional care and within hospitals. If little or no formal training is provided, with few booklets of guidance easily available for care assistants or nurses new to that branch of nursing, then such aspects as privacy and the ability to confer dignity only feature in training on the job, and then only if the senior worker considers it part of their role. It is all much influenced by staff attitudes and individual staff members' discretion and belief in such tasks.

One important aspect of privacy concerns the confused resident or someone with dementia; the more dependent they become, the less control over their privacy they have. There are guides such as those referred to earlier that explain how measures can be identified and used to see if the protections against loss of privacy are being implemented. This includes staff knowledge of residents' expectations regarding personal privacy, acknowledgement of their wishes about being with other people or not, including private space in which to have a conversation, and the opportunity to have a bath or go to the toilet free from intrusion, either accidental or routine. That these measures depend on the cognition of a resident being intact gives some understanding of how difficult it is for staff to ascertain and implement such practices for those with dementia. Here, also, one can observe in terms of privacy, with so many aspects of daily life conducted in public, that residents become irritated by the invasion of their privacy or space by someone with dementia. Residents appear to tolerate such invasions, especially when the person wandering or pacing is pleasant. However, residents say that it becomes intolerable when the behaviour is persistent. Lucid residents often became upset at the constant pacing of one resident, and especially upset at the constant shouting of another. What is tolerated least of all is when a resident finds someone else in her/his bed or bedroom. No matter how understanding she or he tries to be towards the person who cannot find their own bed, this appears to be as difficult an aspect of privacy as having the door opened when sitting on the toilet, which represents the worst type of invasion of personal space as well as an utter sense of disorder.

When considering space, Shirley Ardener (1975: 1) says that a restricted space 'like a club or a nation state has a set of rules to determine how its boundaries shall be crossed and who shall occupy that place'. Likewise, there are unwritten rules concerning boundaries within the nursing home, one hard and fast one being that no one should go into a resident's room unless invited to do so by the occupant. This is where Arthur upset many fellow residents, as he often went in unasked to someone's bedroom. Despite suffering from quite severe dementia, after such occasions he could be reasoned with as long as it was put in terms of 'You can't go into a ladies' room, Arthur'. Written distinctly in his care plan, it was hoped that temporary staff would also be aware of it. As some room doors look very much like the next one, and in terms of boundary around one's own space of a bedroom, this is a difficult area to cope with for residents as well as the staff, especially temporary ones or newcomers. In analysing the image of the English bed and breakfast industry described by Bouquet (1988), Strathern (1992: 129) re-addresses the point made that it is 'the privacy of the home life which is laid out for public consumption'. This resonates with the care home. Strathern says that Bouquet's study showed that although the private domain becomes public, there was yet a further area of privacy that was preserved, an area that no tourist entered. It is this 'inner sanctum' of the resident's bedroom, and especially the bed and personal belongings, that is seen to be inappropriate for other residents to enter and handle. In the public places, the residents are always 'on show' or at least seen by other people, some of whom are not known to them personally. The concept and reality of the care home as a public place, with visitors as well as staff coming and going throughout the day, does little to promote or preserve the notion of it being the residents' 'home from home'.

Here time is also closely associated with space. The timing of washing and dressing for instance, to take place after breakfast, in the intimacy of one's bedroom, contrasts greatly with the open public spaces where the rest of the day will be spent. For the staff, and ultimately those whom they care for, the whole concept of time is pressured, which may well account for why the nurse attended to Albert's urethral catheter in the public space of the lounge instead of his room. To take him to his bedroom would have placed intolerable pressure on the routine. At that time, just before lunch, all residents would be seated in the dining areas awaiting the meal. However, Maddie and Valerie, two care assistants, said that the routine was flexible enough for the nurse to have performed her task in privacy, as they felt that this particular task could have waited until after lunch.

Nowhere is the concept of the total institution more evident in the nursing home than at meal times. The management of meal times seemed to be a bureaucratic exercise in itself, with little evidence of individuality for either the cognitively impaired or cognitively sufficient resident. Only at Christmas was alcohol observed being served with a meal, even though I heard it being requested on a number of occasions. Not once during the meals (except Sundays) was there a relaxed air, just one of rush on the part of the staff, thereby impacting upon the residents. The only evidence of relaxation and quiet was seen during the drinking of tea and coffee served at the tables after the meal itself. Total institution enables the movement of people en masse within institutions, as well as facilitating surveillance. In this home, surveillance is too strong a word to use, but there was an element at meal times of close observation to ensure that the group of people complete the task in hand as a block of people and to order, especially within the constraints of time. A more rigid routine was witnessed here than during any other part of the nursing home day, with the clamour of meal times in particular highlighting an aspect of living that could be changed for the well-being of the residents.

Another characteristic of total institution concerns the restricted inside world of the resident, which contradicts greatly with the freedom of the outside world of the staff and as lived in the memory of the residents. It was, however, the bringing together of two worlds and the building of relationships between staff and residents that made loss of freedom bearable for the resident. Any resentment shown was aimed at management and rarely at staff. As described earlier, care assistants endeavoured to include residents in their own lives and worlds, with the resident being happy to live vicariously through the staff sharing knowledge of family, children, schools, holidays and even problems. This depth of sharing was seen and perceived to come from genuine interaction between the staff member and resident, with staff members saying how fond they were of most of the residents. However, this knowledge was mostly shared while performing tasks with the resident, such as washing or dressing. What was rarely seen was staff sitting with residents during less busy times. Residents said they wished the staff had more time to sit and listen to them, but knew the staff were too busy. However, some of the staff explained that they did not perceive sitting with the residents to be part of their role, as there were often jobs to be completed before going off duty. In that respect, the bringing together of the two worlds was always on their terms and not often when the resident wanted it. Moments when staff stood at either end of the lounge or dining area and talked with all those seated in armchairs or at the dining tables were genuine times of banter, discussion and concern among equals.

Yet another component of Goffman's total institution is that of the newly arrived inmate being stripped of possessions (Goffman 1991: 28). This again is a rather harsh description for what actually takes place in the twenty-first-century institution of a nursing home. There is certainly a sense of loss on the part of many residents on admission to the home, and for many residents the loss of possessions features strongly in aspects of grief. The nursing home management actively encouraged residents to bring possessions in with them, such as a chest of drawers for their room, a pet cat or a bird in a cage. With the help of relatives, many people had personalised their rooms, although this was not always the case. Some of the men's rooms in particular appeared very sparse. The reality is that the rooms are small and many people would have moved from homes they had lived in for years, with all the accumulation of possessions that living in a three-bedroom house or bungalow entails. Where the 'stripping of possessions' became apparent was when a resident was informed or became aware of the selling of her home and furniture. Rosalind was particularly distraught when she knew this was happening, especially as she shared a room as well, which she said felt less than her own. In some respects, residents said they saw the giving up of possessions as part of the approach to death, things only mentioned in the quietness of their own rooms. Not all staff were sensitive to the issue of loss involved, but when they were, they endeavoured to help and encourage the distraught resident by listening to them and allowing them to express their grief and even anger.

The Loneliness of Loss

As already mentioned, people moving into nursing homes have had loss and even multiple losses to deal with concerning their admission. Much as the death of a spouse or significant carer is sad and dealt with by each individual, it is often the loss of a house and, therefore, one's 'home' that is the most significant loss mentioned. Violet's husband said it was the loss 'of normal living' that was unacceptable to both him and his wife, even though she was trying to settle into living in the home. He found it all 'hard to bear', especially their separation, and described her admission in terms of 'abandonment'. If one tries to consider what loss means to people such as Violet and her husband, it is worth considering that the opposite of loss is attachment and that deep and real attachments were made to people, property and possessions in the course of their lifetime. These attachments may have been even deeper if formed in the same vicinity, community or house for forty years or more. Ron, for example, had felt a significant attachment to his greenhouse, spending more time in it than even in his own bungalow; Sybil, the artist, was a regular churchgoer with the same congregation for many years; Eva, the hotelier, had run a lifelong business. What losses the severing of those attachments meant to the people concerned is not fully known, but it is possible that all the attachments were bound up in the notion of 'home'. To lose that solid sense of home was almost like losing the whole notion of life itself.

It must be noted here, though, that there are older people for whom the struggle at home in the community became too much, and for whom the move into the nursing home, with all the losses it entails, was welcomed. The huge amount of energy involved in endeavouring to live at home in the community is often said to be preferable to going into residential care, and is something highlighted by the media. Politicians and DHSS policy statements all stress the need for older people to stay in their own homes, avoiding institutional care. A poignant example recounted by Marge illustrates the kind of struggle involved and her ultimate decision for long-term care. Discharged back home and into community care by social services after a debilitating stroke, Marge relied on five carers at various times of the day to wash and dress her, get a meal ready for her and take her to the toilet. If she needed to go to the toilet at other times than when the carer was present, she was unable to as she could not walk alone, due to her paralysed leg and arm. There are other needs as well; she was unable to get to the light switch one dark winter's afternoon at 3.30 p.m. and had to wait in the dark until the carer came at 5 p.m. Her quality of life living alone diminished significantly enough for her to seriously consider and subsequently decide upon residential care, where she eventually settled.

Imagining and Remembering Home

The importance of the bond between the individual moving into residential care and the home that is being left behind needs to be considered, especially when observing how often it came up in conversation. The phrase 'home from home' was often used by the manager when addressing relatives looking for a nursing home for a family member, or social workers conducting case studies on residents. There is ambivalence about the actual term, but I could see that once used, there could be no other alternative for the manager. It was almost as if by repeating the phrase the manager was creating the notion of a home each time. The positive sides of life in the home were always presented to families and visitors, as well as in publicity brochures, whereas the negative aspects would only be known by staff and residents. Still, how can the nursing home be 'home from home' when for both the resident and the relative so much loss attached to their own home has been experienced? How can it be 'home' when it is also a place of employees and paid work? How can it be 'home' when residents themselves referred to it as 'these kind of places', not as 'home', not even using the name of the institution?

Some residents regularly contested the manager's phrase by saying, 'Of course this is not like home'. In some sense, the question to be asked is, 'Who would agree with the manager that the establishment can actually be a home from home?' The residents would voice the negative aspects of nursing home life after a poor activities session or a particular spate of staff shortage, or an unsuitable meal. Apart from those occasions, which in terms of the activities would often be daily, residents did not always voice negative aspects. Some of those who had a single room were likely to refer to it in terms of the room being 'home' and then indicate that the word 'home' was a 'slip of the tongue'. None who shared a room were heard to call it home. There is a sense of incongruity in sharing a room with someone you do not know, as very few adults in life have had to do this.

Nearly thirty years ago, Willcocks, Peace and Kellaher (1987: 4) were questioning the same use of the word 'home', saying that the

metaphor of domesticity has extensively been used in the residential context with the result that an old people's residence is construed as a home. But the metaphor starts to break down when the distance between home in its traditional sense and home in a residential sense becomes too great.

Adaptation to life in a nursing home does not happen immediately, but is ongoing. Whether the adaptation includes eventually being able to view it as home is debatable, as a form of lifestyle has to be imagined and probably needs to be maintained within such an institution whether it is known as a 'home' or not. Whether buying into a form of lifestyle in the nursing home includes the notion of home may or may not be ascertainable. Many of the residents were prepared to put a brave face on how they really felt about living there and especially how they felt about losing their own home. Along with other commentators on the notion of 'home', Rapport and Dawson (1998) in their exploration of the many ways in which people understand 'home' in the modern era describe the meaning of the word 'home' to be found in the many routines of home life, many relationships, memories and oral narratives within notions of identity.

We can see that missing home or losing their home was bound up with more than just the house itself. It involved cognisant acts of memory, thought and even smell, and a sense of well-being. Looking through greetings cards in most high street chains, one can easily find a card to send as condolence for 'the loss of a pet', which for many was bound up completely with the notion of home, the pet being part of the family. As Waldren (1996: 58) describes in the context of Mallorca, the meaning of '*casa*' incorporates the people or family as well as the house itself, so that '*mi casa*' also means '*mi familia*', my family. The poignancy then of the loss of home for the older person is wrapped up in the loss of family as well, even those with families living near enough to the nursing home to visit. It is the interconnectedness between family, therefore people, and their home as a physical building being emptied and sold that causes the pain and felt loss to the person on moving into the care home, especially when there does not appear to be an alternative solution.

For many of the residents here, their idea of home, even if not put in such terms as conceptual space, was bound up with the relationships of family and friends as well as the community itself, including shops, churches and places of leisure such as public houses and coffee shops. The expectations by family, friends and staff for the resident to adapt to their new setting are almost unbearable for some residents in their early days in the homes. Joan, for example, sat for many days and weeks crying. This research shows that on admission to a residential home, the resident is expected to find the inner resources necessary to face one of the most major adjustments of a lifetime, moving from private living to public communal space. It is not just staff working closely with residents who make these assumptions, but others such as GPs, visitors and especially the person's relatives. This also includes staff other than care assistants and nurses who have contact with the residents, such as kitchen and maintenance staff, domestic and clerical staff.

The term 'nursing home/care home' gives the suggestion of a home-like environment but is in fact a misnomer. Was the manager's effort to create a 'home from home' her attempt to direct the social space and environment of a place that could so easily be just another institution? There is no doubt that the manager tried to personalise the whole setting, evidenced in the way she insisted on having divan beds rather than hospital beds, even for the very sick person. In a guide to standards, *Managing a Home from Home*, Payne (1997) acknowledged that total institutions historically dealt with their patient numbers in a standardised manner, recognising, however, that a more personalised style had begun to be commonplace, and this is certainly evident here. The manager often stressed her hope that attributes of a more personalised way of running a home could actually be seen. It is possible, however, that these personalised characteristics contributing to the idea of 'home from home' that she so desired were in reality a notion of home just too far removed from a lifetime's experiences of home. What this section on the concept of home highlights is that there is evidence of 'home' here and a desired ideal or even imagining of making it a 'home from home' for the residents, which makes it less of the total institution than that described by Goffman.

Linked in with the whole concept of home is what makes up quality of life for the residents in such an institution, and quality of working life for the employee. One of the most significant aspects of quality of life in the nursing home is the presence or absence of respect. Staff who respected residents as people, and not just as a series of assigned tasks to be accomplished within a set number of hours, contributed to their dignity. When considering caring for a person with dementia who has lost the power to express her or himself, respect shown to them enhances the quality of working life for the employee, even if the quality of life for the resident cannot be known. In addition, when management show respect for the staff, there is a more harmonious workforce than when none is shown.

Associated with respect for the resident is the problem of infantilisation of the older person by their carer, whether a relative or a paid carer and other staff members and visitors. We saw in Chapter 2 how the model for caring work as a care assistant comes from that of motherhood and being the family nurturer. Bearing this in mind, it can be seen how infantilisation takes place. One of the most glaring examples observed in the home was the kitchen worker asking Rosalind if she had her 'happy head' on that day or her 'awkward head'. This dialogue can be framed within the whole process of infantilisation associated with the social discourse on ageing. Infantilisation shapes people's experiences in a powerful way, especially with emotions such as vulnerability and the social marginalisation of living on the periphery. When staff respect residents as people, they enable them to live full if dependent lives, whereas when they do not respect them as people, and when in particular they transform them into children to be cared for, they are denying them their very personhood. On a number of occasions, residents were heard to mumble, 'I'm not a kid you know'. This notion of transforming an adult into a dependent child is both disempowering and marginalising in terms of muteness, where the dominant group, here seen as the workforce, mutes and even silences the seemingly less powerful frail older person. When one of the male residents, Tom, felt unable to voice his despair at being treated like a child, on being served fish fingers for his main meal during the beef ban, his despair and his muteness led him to try and take his own life. Although there were other factors in his life making him feel life was not worth living, on more than one occasion this able-bodied retired farmer in his mid-eighties expressed how he felt the serving of fish fingers to be humiliating and demoralising. Infantilisation of older people can happen when staff without professional training, who are professionally unsure of themselves, find it advantageous to establish a parent–child relationship rather than an adult–adult one. This infantilisation happens when residents are treated like children by staff who cannot or will not consider the residents' achievements over a lifetime, their biography as it were. Tom, in particular, knew more about the meat industry and farming than either management or the homeowners, and felt from his life's experience that the ban on serving beef was unnecessary and that the choice should have been left to them as adults.

Throughout the 1990s, I noticed a correlation between the symptoms of Creutzfeldt-Jakob Disease (CJD) and certain symptoms of dementia. It was interesting to me that the nursing home studied was located in a rural area, with a number of residents admitted from farming communities where the Bovine Spongiform Encephalopathy (BSE) crisis had occurred. I thought that a number of residents showing symptoms diagnosed as dementia may, on post-mortem investigation of brain biopsy, prove to correlate with a diagnosis of CJD. Tom the farmer felt able to discuss his farming career and knowledge of beef production with me, suggesting that farmers had as much clinical knowledge, if not more, of their cattle than the government agricultural officers. The truth of this correlation has since been shown by others including Judith Okely (1999), who upon the death of her mother, who had been diagnosed with dementia, requested a brain biopsy, which showed the conclusive presence of the CJD infectious agent known as a prion.

Inactivity and Its Impact on Low Morale

When observing activity in the nursing home, whether self-motivated or provided by the activities leader, the frailty and age of many residents must be considered. On first sight, in any of the three lounges, many people appeared to be just sitting doing nothing. A number of residents said they were content just to sit with people they had got to know since moving into the home. Some of the frailest or most sick, such as Sybil and Maisie, did not often speak but appeared happy just to sit quietly. It was the more-able bodied residents who often voiced their protests at long hours of sitting with nothing to do. In the 1950s and 1960s, Townsend's (1964) ground-breaking study of old people's homes showed an overall impression of sitting around and inactivity. He found that communal homes in England and Wales did not adequately meet the physical, psychological and social needs of the people living in them. In the present study, the voices of protest from residents were loudest when these needs were not addressed. A significant factor observed was the way contentment among the residents could be seen in terms of activities and relief from boredom, whereas hours of inactivity produced dissatisfaction. Because there had been a history of good occupa-tional activities in the afternoons in the home here studied, the dissatisfac-tion with poor ones was noticeable. An important issue related by many residents was that they would prefer their social needs to be met before those concerning their physical environment. Even standards of care were not felt by the resident to be as important as the quality of their relationships. One can place activity sessions within the domain of social relationships and social discourse as it is during these group settings that much verbal interac-tion and affectionate tactile gestures take place. When the activities session was deemed to be 'poor' by the participants, therefore, it also affected their desired opportunities for social interaction with other residents and staff as well as raising or lowering their morale. Poor quality or poorly thought out social activities were seen to be not only boring but demeaning to the person concerned, which links in closely with the notion of respect and dignity illustrated earlier. The way that Wynona, Edwina and others expressed their low morale, sometimes on a daily basis, was discussed by care assistants in particular, who at times expressed their surprise at the activities leader apparently not being aware of this. However, the care assistants said they did not feel able to discuss this with her personally. Fifty years after Townsend's research, there is still room to enhance the daily quality of lived life for older people in residential homes.

Quality of Life for Residents and Employees

Many factors influenced the quality of life experienced by residents in the nursing home, one of the most important being the degree of frailty and immobility that a person had to come to terms with, especially as their frailty increased. Lifelong individual coping strategies were shown by residents, but these were seen to be less effective when coping with hours of inactivity. The multiple losses experienced before and after admission to the home signified a felt decline in the quality of life for the individual concerned, as illustrated by the male resident stressing how he dearly missed being able to go to his greenhouse. Little in the nursing home could make up for that loss, although he did endeavour to get involved in activities sessions when offered to him. Only the individual can determine the presence of quality of life, but there is an ongoing need to ensure that attention by staff is given to this concept. Certain conditions should be met that could confirm the presence of quality of life, particularly an emphasis on stimulus and conversations resulting from relationships with others.

As shown in Chapter 2, residents were grateful for the ways in which care assistants cared for them, especially as they became more dependent upon their help. However, when staff shortages led to a perceived decline in attention to detail within that care, residents would be vocal in their criticism of the situation. Quality of life for both resident and the care assistant was shown to be inextricably linked. In particular, the minutiae of detail held the attention of some of the residents, who became upset for instance at having morning tea consistently served to them slopped in the saucer. A cup of tea served hot and not 'slopped' was commented upon without fail, indicating how important such small details of life were. Residents were seen to be upset if things were done in ways that they felt were not correct, such as having a banana cut up on a place-mat instead of on a plate, as described earlier. These kinds of incidents confirmed to the resident that they were part of institutional life, which they felt did not contain the same qualities as 'being at home'. Meal times in particular and the eating habits of other residents impacted upon their perceived desires that make up individual satisfaction and therefore quality of life. The speed at which meal times were conducted observes the loss of individuality for the resident in the rush on the part of the staff to get the job done.

If this attention to detail is part of the make-up of quality of life, can it be used to define quality of life? What is being aimed for within the concept of quality of life are essentials other than those required for mere existence, such as being fed, clothed and being free from danger. Here what makes up quality of life was seen to be especially dependent upon relationships, particularly those formed by the resident with the care assistant. This corroborates what Peace, Hall and Hamblin (1979) highlighted, and especially Goffman's (1991) and Townsend's (1964) findings, namely that residents in a residential home are isolated from their previous world. The formation of new relationships, especially those with the care assistants, is more than a coping strategy – it becomes part of the foundation for new friendships. Within this perceived isolation, as highlighted in Chapter 4, there is a consistent need for quality activities and stimuli to relieve the tedium of life in a nursing home, and in particular some relief from the memories of the losses encountered, especially loss of relationships with family, friends and neighbours.

One of the major criteria within a definition of quality of life for care home residents, therefore, is that of stimulus. That these stimuli can be written into the daily routine is evidenced in the undertaking of good activities sessions and outings. But more than this is needed for the resident to sense that she is part of everyday life. Conversation with employees and visitors, anticipated eagerly and shared with other residents, is the stimulus necessary to enable frail, sick people to feel that they can take part in other people's lives and not just the somewhat isolating life of a home. Freedom from the boredom of inactivity is seen as a significant and necessary component of satisfactory quality of life. There is a general expectation on the part of the resident that they will be involved in arranged activities and the anticipated stimulus. In particular, it was shown that people with dementia do respond to stimuli and that cognitive and social stimulation, even within the routine of the home, is seen to be an important prerequisite for the enjoyment of life.

In endeavouring to define quality of life for people living in a home, the whole sum should be an actual and representational experience of the life that the person has left behind. It seems to be determined by the presence and importance of certain characteristics, such as relationships between resident and care assistant, and these are most significant. Other significant relationships are between resident and any remaining family and friends; resident and resident does not feature so highly. Also of importance is the continuation of practices that reflect something of the life lived before admission. This includes attention to details of hygiene, such as washing and dressing in one's own clothes. Privacy and a sense of one's own space in the midst of a public place are seen to be significant characteristics necessary in the make-up of a meaningful quality of life in the nursing home setting.

It is evident from these characteristics that make up quality of life in any nursing home that they pertain to that individual establishment. However, by listening to the voices of the people therein, it would appear that these characteristics represent components for a definition of quality of life to be applied to all institutions, emanating from a deep social need within all. The absence or presence of quality of life, as seen in the case studies and heard in the oral narratives of residents and staff, is a difficult concept to define, elusive even. Aspects of it are either present or not when considering such questions as routine and disorder examined earlier. Issues around the actual event of admission have much to do with immense loss within a person's life and can contribute to the felt lack of quality of life, possibly for many months afterwards, if not forever. Attention to privacy and private and public space impacts on the physical environment of the resident, as well as their psychological need for privacy, to such an extent that their whole experience of life in the home can be adversely affected. When nursing home employees such as care assistants feel valued and of worth as individuals, to management in particular, this is shown to affect not only their lives but the lives of the people they care for. Only when management and staff actually listen to what older people are saying and pay close attention to the way in which 'home' is defined by the residents, their relatives and society itself, will the remnants of Goffman's 'total institution' finally disappear.

GLOSSARY

ﮯﺑﮯﺑﮯ

ADLs	activities of daily living
ADS	Alzheimer's Disease Society
Alpha FIM	Alpha Functional Independence Measure
BSE	Bovine Spongiform Encephalopathy
CJD	Creutzfeldt-Jakob Disease
CORC	The Commission on Residential Care
CPN	Community Psychiatric Nurse
DHSS	Department of Health and Social Security
DVLA	Driver Vehicle Licensing Centre
GCSE	General Certificate of Secondary Education
GP	General Practitioner (doctor)
NHS	National Health Service
NVQ	National Vocational Qualification
OUH	Oxford University Hospital Trust
RCN	Royal College of Nursing
UTI	urinary tract infection
WC	lavatory

BIBLIOGRAPHY

Abbott, R.A., R. Whear, J. Thompson-Coon, O.C. Ukoumunne, M. Rogers, A. Bethel, A. Hemsley and K. Stein. 2013. 'Effectiveness of Mealtime Interventions on Nutritional Outcomes for the Elderly Living in Residential Care: A Systematic Review and Meta-analysis', *Ageing Research Reviews* 12: 967–81.

Abraham, A. 2011. 'NHS Has Failed Elderly, Says Damning Report', *The Times*, 15 February.

Age UK. 2015. *Later Life in the United Kingdom*, fact sheet.

Alzheimer, A. 1907. 'Uber eine eigenartige Erkrankung der Hirnrinde', *Allgemeine Zeitschrift fur Psychiatrie und phychash-Gerichtliche Medizin* 64: 146–48.

Alzheimer's Disease Society. 1998. *Submission to the Royal Commission on Long-Term Care for Older People*. London: ADS.

Alzheimer's Disease Society. 2014. 'Dementia 2014 Report Statistics'. Retrieved 1 December 2015 from https://www.alzheimers.org.uk/statistics.

Alzheimer's Disease Society. 2016. 'About Dementia: Eating and Drinking'. Retrieved 19 October 2016 from https://www.alzheimers.org.uk/site/scripts/documents_info.php?documentID=149.

Aneshensel, C., L.I. Pearlin, J.T. Mullan, S.H. Zarit and C.S. Whitlach. 1995. *Profiles in Caregiving: The Unexpected Career*. San Diego: Academic Press.

Ansdell, G. 2015. *How Music Helps in Music Therapy and Everyday Life*. Farnham: Ashgate.

Archibald, C. 1994. *Sexuality and Dementia: A Guide*. Stirling: Dementia Services Development Centre, University of Stirling.

Ardener, E. 1975. 'The Problem Revisited', in S. Ardener (ed.), *Perceiving Women*. London: J.M. Dent & Sons Ltd, pp. 19–27.

Ardener, S. (ed.). 1975. *Perceiving Women*. London: J.M. Dent & Sons Ltd.

Ardener, S. (ed.). 1993. *Defining Females: The Nature of Women in Society*. Oxford: Berg.

Arnold, P., H. Bochel, S. Brodhurst and D. Page. 1993. *Community Care: The Housing Dimension*. York: Joseph Rowntree Foundation.

Aslet, C. 1994. 'Where Do I Want to Live When I'm Old?', *The Times*, 27 October.

Barrow, M., and S. Coates. 2012. 'Councils Still Measuring Elderly Care in Minutes', *The Times*, 26 March.

Bauley, J. 2012. 'The Elderly Are Not Bed Blockers They Are Patients', *The Times*, 18 April.

Bayley, J. 1997. 'A Time of Tranquil Ceremony', *The Times*, 24 December.

Bennett, R. 2012a. 'Transform Care for the Elderly, Urge Charities', *The Times*, 1 June.

Bennett, R. 2012b. 'No. 10 Sits on 'Urgent' Care Reforms', *The Times*, 12 July.

Bennett, R. 2012c. '250,000 Elderly Britons Alone and Lonely at Christmas', *The Times*, 29 November.

Bennett, R. 2013. 'Overstretched Care Workers 'Put Elderly in Danger', *The Times*, 8 October.

Bennett, R. 2014. 'Old People Turn to 'Lonely' Care Homes Only as a Final Resort', *The Times*, 3 September.

Blakeley, R. 2012. 'Put Our Parents Out to Grass in Hi-tech Garden Shed', *The Times*, 1 December.

Bouquet, M. 1988. 'All Modern Conveniences: Properties of Home Comfort in English Farmhouse Accommodation', Paper presented at the *Anthropology of Tourism Conference*, London, 22–23 April 1988.

Buchannan, Maura, 2014. Former President, Royal College of Nursing, personal communication.

Butler, M. 1996. *Worship in Residential Care*. Derby: Christian Council on Aging.

Cicero. 1923. *De Senectute*, trans. W.A. Falconer. Cambridge, MA: Harvard University Press.

Counsel and Care. 1992. *Managing a Home from Home*. London: Counsel and Care.

Cox, J. 1995. 'Woman of 79 Has Paid £100,000 for Husband's Nursing', *The Times*, 7 August.

de Beauvoir, S. 1977. *Old Age*. London: Penguin.

DEMOS. 2014. *The Commission on Residential Care, 2014*. London: DEMOS.

Denney, A. 1997. 'Quiet Music: An Intervention for Mealtime Agitation?' *Journal of Gerontological Nursing* 23(7): 16–23.

Department of Health. 1990. *National Health Service and Community Care Act 1990*. London: HMSO.

Dewing, J., and P. Garner. 1998. 'Listening to Enid', *Elder Care* 10(4): 12–15.

Diamond, T. 1992. *Making Gray Gold: Narratives of Nursing Home Care*. Chicago: University of Chicago Press.

Dickinson, A., and S. Kendall 1996. 'The Nutritional Status of the Elderly Population in the UK: A Systematic Review and Implications for Primary Health Care', *Research Reports in Nursing and Health*. Chalfont St Giles: Buckinghamshire College.

Dilnot, A., N. Warner and J. Williams. 2011. *The Report of the Commission on Funding of Caring and Support*, Vol. 1: Fairer Care Funding. Retrieved 8 March 2016 from http//www.dilnotcommission.dh.gov.uk.

Douglas, M. 1966. *Purity and Danger: An Analysis of the Concepts of Pollution and Taboo*. London: Ark Paperbacks.

Editor. 1995. 'Scheme Helps Elderly Stay Put', *Oxford Mail*, 20 February.

Editor. 2013. 'Care Home Measures May Not Halt Crisis', *The Times*, 13 February.

Editorial. 1995. 'A Tax on Caring', *The Times*, 17 June.

Editorial. 1997. 'Protection for the Elderly', *The Sunday Times*, 12 October.

Editorial. 1999. 'Care Free: A Royal Commission of Royal Extravagance', *The Times*, 2 March.

Editorial. 2011. 'Without Care', *The Times*, 1 August.

Editorial. 2014. 'Barely Legal', *The Times*, 15 May.

Editorial. 2015. 'Elderly Care Home Residents Auctioned off by Councils on "eBay-Style" Website', *Daily Telegraph*, 9 February.

Elias, N. 1939. *The Civilising Process: The History of Manners*. Oxford: Basil Blackwell Publishers Ltd.

Elliott, V. 1999. 'Garden Where Memories Grow', *The Times*, 1 June.

Evers, H. 1981. 'Care or Custody? The Experience of Women Patients in Long-Stay Geriatric Wards', in B. Hutter and G. Williams (eds), *Controlling Women: The Normal and the Deviant*. London: Croom Helm with Oxford University Women Studies Committee, pp. 108–130.

Foner, N. 1994. *The Caregiving Dilemma: Work in an American Nursing Home*. Berkeley: University of California.

Ford. R. 2011. 'Midlifers Caught between Worlds', *The Times*, 23 September.

Foucault, M. 1961. *Madness and Civilisation: A History of Insanity in the Age of Reason*. Translation into English, 1967. London: Routledge.

Foucault, M. 1988. 'On Power', in L.D. Kritzman (ed.), *Michel Foucault, Politics, Philosophy, Culture: Interviews and Other Writings, 1977–1984*. New York: Routledge, pp. 96–109.

Frean, A. 1999. 'Let the Old Eat What They Want, Says Leith', *The Times*, 9 June.

Garbedian, C. 2014. 'I'd Rather Have Music! The Effects of Live and Recorded Music for People with Dementia Living in Care Homes and Their Carers', Ph.D. thesis. Stirling: University of Stirling.

Geertz, C. 1973. *The Interpretation of Cultures*. London: Fontana.

Goffman, E. 1961. *Asylums: Essays on the Social Situation of Mental Patients and Other Inmates*. 1991 edition. London: Penguin.

Grant, L. 1997. 'What the Eyes Don't See', *The Guardian*, 20 May.

Hinkle, J.L., J. McClaran, J. Davies and D. Ng. 2010. 'Reliability and Validity of the Adult Alpha Functional Independence Measure Instrument in England', *Journal of Neuroscience Nursing* 42(1): 12–18.

Hochschild, A.R. 1989. *The Second Shift: Working Parents and the Revolution at Home*. London: Platkus.

Hockey, J., and A. James. 1993. *Growing Up and Growing Old: Aging and Dependency in the Life Course*. London: Sage.

Horsnell, M. 1995. 'Granny Flats to be Charged Council Tax', *The Times*, 17 June.

Jacques, A. 1992. *Understanding Dementia*, 2nd edn. Edinburgh: Churchill Livingstone.

Kane, F., and J. Waples. 1994. 'Home Sweet Home', *The Sunday Times*, 4 December.

Kayser-Jones, J. 1981. *Old, Alone and Neglected: Care of the Aged in Scotland and the United States*. Berkeley: University of California Press.

Kayser-Jones, J. 1996. 'Mealtime in Nursing Homes: The Importance of Individualized Care', *Journal of Gerontological Nursing* 22(3): 26–31.

Kelly, M. 1993. *Designing for People with Dementia in the Context of Building Standards*. Stirling: Dementia Services Development Centre, University of Stirling.

Kovach, C.R., and H. Henschel. 1996. 'Planning Activities for Patients with Dementia: A Descriptive Study of Therapeutic Activities on Special Care Units', *Journal of Gerontological Nursing* 22(9): 33–38.

Lamb, N. 2014. 'Care Bill Becomes Care Act 2014'. Retrieved 1 July 2014 from https://www.gov.uk/government/speeches/care-bill-becomes-care-act-2014.

Laurance, J. 'Families Given Warning on Costs of Care', *The Times*, 24 February.

Law, V. 2013. 'Plenty of Reasons to Laugh in this Happy, Loving Home', *The Times*, 2 December.

Lay, K. 2016. 'Woman Cannot Find Care Home after Allegations of Ill Treatment', *The Times*, 11 January.

Lee-Treweek, G. 1997. 'Women, Resistance and Care: Nursing Auxiliary Work', *Work, Employment and Society* 11(1): 47–63.

Letters to the Editor. 2011. 'Care for the Elderly is a Casualty of Over-Pressed Nursing', *The Times*, 16 February.

Letters to the Editor. 2012a. 'Dutch Approach to Dementia is Encouraging', *The Times*, 7 April.

Letters to the Editor. 2012b. 'Reality of Caring for Elderly Relatives in 21st-Century Britain', *The Times*, 17 May.

Lidz, C.W., L. Fischer and R.M. Arnold. 1992. *The Erosion of Autonomy in Long-Term Care*. New York: Oxford University Press.

Lin Gu. 2015. 'Nursing Interventions in Managing Wandering Behaviour in Patients with Dementia: A Literature Review', *Archives of Psychiatric Nursing* 29: 454–57.

Local Government Association. 2014. 'Care Act Reforms'. Retrieved 1 September 2014 from http://www.communitycare.co.uk/2014/08/27/five-ways-social-workers-want-care-act-guidance-strengthened/.

Maclean, R. 2012. 'Music Offers a Path Back to Reality for Dementia Sufferers', *The Times*, 3 January.

Mali, J. 2008. 'Comparison of the Characteristics of Homes for Older People in Slovenia with Goffman's Concept of the Total Institution', *European Journal of Social Work* 11(4): 431–43.

Menzies, I.E.P. 1970. *The Functioning of Social Systems as a Defence against Anxiety*. London: Tavistock Institute of Human Relations.

Miller, E. 2016. 'Beyond Bingo', *Journal of Leisure Research* 48(1): 35–49.

Miller, J. 1998. 'Assault on the Mind: A Commentary', Documentary, Channel 4, April.

Ministerio de Asuntos Sociales. 1996. *Llar de Majors de Calvia: Viure como a ca teva*. Calvia: Ajuntament de Calvia Mallorca.

Moody, O. 2012. 'Elderly 'Would Rather Lose Fuel Cash than Bus Passes', *The Times*, 13 October.

Mulley, G., C. Bowman, M. Boyd and S. Stowe (eds). 2015. *The Care Home Handbook*. Oxford: Wiley Blackwell.

Murphey, C.M. 1988. *Day to Day: Spiritual Help When Someone You Love Has Alzheimer's*. Philadelphia: The Westminster Press.

Murray, I., and N. Wood. 1995. 'Battle to Stop Elderly Losing their Homes', *The Times*, 7 August.

Okely, J. 1994. 'Vicarious and Sensory Knowledge of Chronology and Change: Ageing in Rural France', in K. Hastrup and P. Hervik (eds), *Social Experience and Anthropological Knowledge*. London: Routledge, pp. 34–48.

Okely, J. 1996. *Own or Other Culture*. London: Routledge.

Okely, J. 1999. 'Love, Care and Diagnosis', in T. Kohn and R. McKechnie (eds), *Extending the Boundaries of Care: Medical Ethics and Caring Practices*. Oxford: Berg, pp. 19–48.

Papastavrou, E., A. Kalokerinou, S.S. Papacostas, H. Tsangari and P. Sourtzi. 2007. 'Caring for a Relative with Dementia: Family Caregiver Burden', *Journal of Advanced Nursing* 58(5): 446–57.

Payne, C. 1997. *Managing a Home from Home: Guide to Standards*. London: Residential Forum.

Peace, S.M., J.F. Hall and G.R. Hamblin. 1979. 'The Quality of Life of the Elderly in Residential Care', *Research Report No. 1*. London: Survey Research Unit, Polytechnic of North London.

Peace, S.M., L.A. Kellaher and D.M. Willcocks. 1982. *A Balanced Life? A Consumer Study of Residential Life in One Hundred Local Authority Old People's Homes*. London: Survey Research Unit, Polytechnic of North London.

Peace, S., L.A. Kellaher and D.M. Willcocks. 1997. *Re-evaluating Residential Care*. Buckingham: Open University Press.

Phillipson, C. 1982. *Capitalism and the Construction of Old Age*. London: Macmillan.

Philpot, T. 2008. *Residential Care: A Positive Future*. New Malden: Residential Forum.

Purves, L. 2011. 'Strategic Vision Won't Fix a Leaky Lavatory', *The Times*, 8 August.

Rapport, N., and A. Dawson (eds). 1998. *Migrants of Identity: Perceptions of Home in a World of Movement*. Oxford: Berg.

Residential Forum. 1996. *Creating a Home from Home: A Guide to Standards*. London: Residential Forum.

Rickford, F. 1997. 'Gently, Gingerly...', *The Guardian*, 5 February.

Royal College of Nursing. 1998. 'Evidence from the Royal College of Nursing to the Royal Commission on Long-Term Care', *Elder Care* 10(3): 6–11.

Royal Commission on Long-Term Care for the Elderly. 1999. *With Respect to Old Age: Long-Term Care – Rights and Responsibilities*. London: Stationery Office. Retrieved 1 July 2014 from http://www.archive.official-documents.co.uk/document/cm41/4192/4192.htm

Savage, M. 2011. 'Spending on Care for the Elderly Falls by a Fifth', *The Times*, 28 October.

Scott, O. 2012. 'What Shall We Do With Mother?', *The Times 2*, 13 July.

Sherman, J., and A. Frean. 1995. 'Elderly Must Wait on Care', *The Times*, 2 March.

Smyth, C. 2012. 'Stop Sending Patients Home Late at Night, Hospitals Told', *The Times*, 17 April.

Smyth, C. 2013a. 'Cruel Short Visits Deprive Elderly of Dignity and Care', *The Times*, 7 October.

Smyth, C. 2013b. 'Heston Helps Older Patients Get a Healthy Appetite Back', *The Times*, 23 December.

Strathern, M. 1992. *After Nature: English Kinship in the Late Twentieth Century*. Cambridge: Cambridge University Press.

Suzman, M., and M. Rich. 1996. 'Nursing Home Operators Look for Healthier Future', *Financial Times*, 4 May.

Thomas, D. 1952. *In Country Sleep, and Other Poems*. London: Dent.

Thompson, A. 2013. 'Who Will Look After You When You Are Old?', *The Times*, 9 October.

Townsend, P. 1964. *The Last Refuge*. London: Routledge and Kegan Paul.

Waldren, J. 1996. *Insiders and Outsiders: Paradise and Reality in Mallorca*. Oxford: Berghahn Books.

Willcocks, D., S. Peace and L. Kellaher. 1987. *Private Lives in Public Places: A Research Based Critique of Residential Life in Local Authority Old People's Homes*. London: Tavistock Publications.

Wilson, F. 2015. 'It's Horrible to Say, but Dementia Is a Writer's Gift', *The Times 2*, 6 January 2015.

INDEX

New Directions in Anthropology

General Editor: **Jacqueline Waldren**, *Institute of Social and Cultural Anthropology, University of Oxford*

Twentieth-century migration, modernization, technology, tourism, and global communication have had dynamic effects on group identities, social values and conceptions of space, place, and politics. This series features new and innovative ethnographic studies concerned with these processes of change.